Spain Is Different

Spain Is Different

Second Edition

HELEN WATTLEY-AMES

INTERCULTURAL PRESS, INC.

First published by Intercultural Press. For information, contact:

Intercultural Press, Inc.
PO Box 700
Yarmouth, Maine 04096, USA
Tel: 207-846-5168
Fax: 207-846-5181
www.interculturalpress.com

Nicholas Brealey Publishing
3-5 Spafield Street
London, EC1R 4QB, UK
Tel: +44-207-239-0360
Fax: +44-207-239-0370
www.nbrealey-books.com

Cover Design: Patty J. Topel
Book Production: Patty J. Topel

Printed in the United States of America

06 05 04 03 02   4 5 6 7 8

Library of Congress Cataloging-in-Publication Data

Wattley-Ames, Helen
    Spain is different/Helen Wattley-Ames—2nd. ed.
        p.   cm.   — (InterAct series)
    Includes bibliographical references.
    ISBN 1-877864-71-4
    1. National characteristics, Spanish. I. Title. II. Series.
DP52.W38 1999
946—dc21   98-46405
                                                          CIP

For my parents,
George and Margaret Wattley

Table of Contents

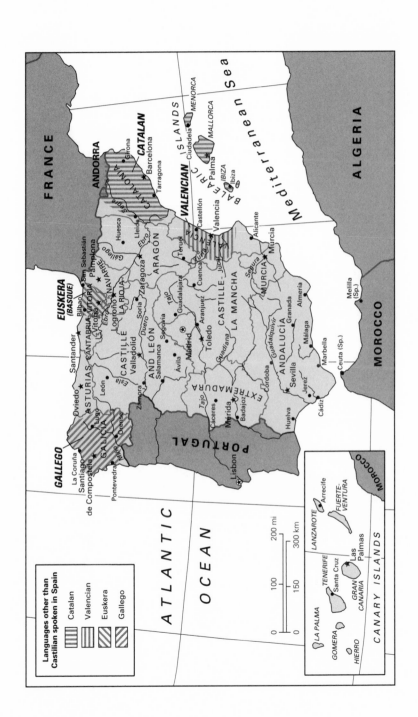

FRANCE

ANDORRA

CATALAN

CATALUÑA

Girona
Barcelona
Tarragona

VALENCIAN ISLANDS

MENORCA

MALLORCA

Ciudadela

Palma
IBIZA
Ibiza

BALEARIC

Mediterranean Sea

ALGERIA

Bilbao
San Sebastián
EUSKERA
(BASQUE)
Pamplona
NAVARRE
Vitoria

Huesca

Lleida

Sabero

Ebro

ARAGÓN

Castellón

Valencia

VALENCIA

Alicante

Murcia

MURCIA

Almería

Granada

Málaga

Marbella

Ceuta (Sp.)

Melilla
(Sp.)

MOROCCO

Santander
Oviedo
ASTURIAS
CANTABRIA
Logroño
LA RIOJA
Zaragoza
Ebro
Soria
Guadalajara
Cuenca
Júcar
Teruel

Júcar

Segura

Jalón

Santiago
de Compostela
La Coruña

GALLEGO

GALICIA

Lugo

Orense

Miño

Pontevedra

Esla

León

Zamora

Gállego

Valladolid

CASTILLE
AND LEÓN

Duero

Salamanca

Ávila

Segovia

Madrid

Aranjuez

Toledo

Tajo

CASTILLE-
LA MANCHA

Guadiana

Córdoba

ANDALUCÍA

Guadalquivir

Sevilla

Jerez

Huelva

Cádiz

EXTREMADURA

Cáceres

Mérida

Badajoz

Tajo

PORTUGAL

Lisbon

ATLANTIC

OCEAN

0   100   200 mi

0   150   300 km

Languages other than
Castilian spoken in Spain

Catalan

Valencian

Euskera

Gallego

MOROCCO

LANZAROTE
Arrecife
FUERTE-
VENTURA

LA PALMA
TENERIFE
Santa Cruz
GOMERA
GRAN
CANARIA
Las
Palmas
HIERRO

CANARY ISLANDS

Preface

Many Americans focused on Spain for the first time in 1992. That year saw the five-hundredth anniversary of Spain's arrival in the New World, the Olympic Games in Barcelona, and the World's Fair in Seville. The significant economic development of Spain during recent years and its active participation in the European Community have also attracted new interest from American companies in a variety of industries.

Business personnel, diplomats, students, athletes, and other visitors going to Spain are discovering the truth of an early slogan of the country's tourist industry: Spain is different. Although this phrase has sometimes been used when comparing Spain negatively with other countries, its original intention was to celebrate the special identity of Spain, its culture and its people.

In this book, a volume in the InterAct series, we focus on the culture and the people and pay special attention to the particular ways in which these differ from the culture and people of the United States. This InterAct, like the others, explores the different histories through which the two peoples have lived and the distinctive values they hold. Their perceptions and expectations of each other are examined. Different ways of thinking, acting, and interacting in both social and work situations are explained. Examples are given of how the words and actions of a person from one culture impress, frustrate, motivate, or embarrass someone from the other. Points of potential conflict are anticipated, and specific guidelines are offered to help ensure mutual understanding and cooperation.

Our purpose is to enable each person who reads an InterAct to be more confident in approaching the foreign culture and more competent in communicating with its people. Better relationships can then be developed and major goals can be achieved. Americans who travel to the country can become more perceptive observers and respectful (as well as respected) guests. Americans who live there will be better equipped to become more successful competitors, contributing colleagues, or trusted friends.

We asked our own colleague and friend, Helen Wattley-Ames, to write this book because she has lived in Barcelona, Spain, where she worked at the Instituto de Estudios Norteamericanos from 1982 to 1987 and experienced first-hand the interaction of Spaniards and Americans. Helen is fluent in Spanish, having received her bachelor's degree in Spanish language and literature at the University of Bristol, England. She comes from Trinidad and Tobago, a country with a Spanish heritage of its own.

In preparing the first edition of this book, Helen interviewed a range of carefully selected Spaniards and Americans in Spain who were keenly aware of the differences between the two cultures and the difficulties they experienced in cross-cultural interaction. Now, revised and updated and enriched by further research, *Spain Is Different* continues to offer the reader striking insights into Spanish culture and how to interact successfully with the Spaniards one encounters—in Spain or elsewhere.

—George W. Renwick
Editor, InterAct series

Acknowledgments

I am grateful to all the people who answered questions and read and commented on the manuscript of this book:

Carlos Alcabés, Joan Azulay, Rick Azulay, Pedro Beltrán, José María Bonsoms, Carmen Canes, Michael Chandler, Carlos Conde, Laurie Derechin, Robert Friedman, Ron Green, Sue Hershelman, John Hunter, Nora Ligorano, Gabriel Lluch, Connie Luff, Rosa María Malet, Robert Maple, Gloria Moure, Joaquin Muns, Marshall Reese, Francisco Sánchez, Neus Silva, Mike Vaal, Enrique Vidal-Ribas and Silvia Vidal-Ribas.

The past and present editors and production team at Intercultural Press.

Special thanks to Bill Ames for all his support.

1

Spain Is Different

What Is Spain?

Regional Differences

Spain is a large country (by European standards), characterized by marked regional differences more substantial than variations in local cuisine or folk music.

Geographically, it might be said that Spain faces in four directions: toward the Atlantic, toward Europe, toward the Mediterranean, and toward Africa. The climate varies accordingly. Andalucía, in the south, has a North African climate with mild winters and extremely hot summers. The center of the country is high plateau (*meseta*) and is quite arid, with little forest cover and extreme temperature variation. The Mediterranean coast, known as *Levante*, is neither as hot as Andalucía nor as cold as the meseta. Galicia and Cantabria, in the northwest, are lush and green from the copious rainfall from the Atlantic. The Pyrenees, Spain's northern boundary with Europe, are snow-covered much of the year, and the valleys of the foothills are covered with pine forests and flowering meadows.

The regions of Spain are also historically different from one another. It is said that all the peoples of southern Europe came to Spain and stayed. To the original Celts and Iberians have been added Carthaginians, Romans, Goths, North Africans, and others. Although the Moors, as North African Muslims are usually called in Spain, at one time overran almost all of the country (except the Basque areas in the north), the degree of their influence varied. Throughout Spain, architecture that bears the mark of Moorish influence can be seen, but it was in Andalucía, where they ruled for nearly eight hundred years, that the Moors left their most indelible imprint. The people, architecture, and lifestyle of Andalucía are those most commonly seen by foreigners as typically Spanish. The northeastern region of Catalonia had more links with southern France and with parts of Italy. Catalonia, the Basque country, Cantabria, and Galicia were the first parts of Spain to be "reconquered" from the Moors and to develop their own systems of social organization, so the Muslim influence is much less evident here than in Andalucía.

The diversity of Spain's regions is recognized in the Constitution of 1978, in which autonomous regions were established with separate governmental and, to a certain extent, financial structures, comparable in many ways to the federal system of the United States.

In terms of identity and loyalty, consciousness of region is probably stronger in Spain than consciousness of country. In the United States national patriotism is far more important than regional loyalty because the concept of the nation was one of the links that held together a country of radically disparate peoples, spread over a sparsely settled continent. Thus, national loyalty has traditionally been a public virtue, expressed by flags in front yards and the daily pledge of allegiance in schools. Events such as the Gulf War and even the Olympic Games are often hyped by American media into patriotic celebrations.

Spain's participation in NATO and United Nations peace-keeping operations and in the Barcelona Olympics were also sources of national pride. But Spaniards are more likely, in international events, to share the limelight rather than monopolize it.

In Spain, the imposition of nationhood upon existing smaller nations has left the country with strong regional identities that have persisted despite the efforts of successive central governments to dilute them. The regime of General Francisco Franco (1939–75) suppressed regional languages and fostered migration between regions (notably, from Andalucía to Catalonia). Further, national patriotism during the Franco era took on unfortunate connotations when it was equated with xenophobic policies or what amounted to complacent isolationism. In reaction to this recent history, regional governments now direct their efforts toward regional nationalism, especially through cultural policies that foster the language, traditions, literature, and arts of the region, often to the detriment of a national perspective.

Spaniards as well as outsiders are concerned about the degree to which local governments overdo regional nationalism. Years ago, the Catalan writer Miquel Llor coined the name Comarquinal for a fictional city that represented the worst in small-minded provincialism (the equivalent of Sinclair Lewis's Gopher Prairie in *Main Street*). It is not hard to find signs of this provincialism in regional attitudes—in the policy, for example, of a major orchestra not to hire players from other regions of Spain, even if it means hiring foreigners instead.

Strong regional identities are not unique to Spain. Other European countries such as France, Germany, Italy, and the United Kingdom also have clearly defined regional differences. Time will tell if regionalism will be diluted or strengthened by greater regional autonomy.

Language Diversity

Spain is also diverse linguistically. Gallego, spoken in Galicia, is akin to Portuguese. Euskera, spoken by the Basques, is a unique language which linguists have never been able to connect to another language family. Suggested origins range from Atlantis to the lost tribes of Israel. Catalan is the language of Catalonia, and Valencian (closely related to Catalan) is spoken in the province of Valencia.

These languages are taught in school and given equal status with Castilian—native to Castile and the official language of Spain—in the respective regions. Visitors must be ready and willing to deal with bilingualism in the people they encounter. Foreigners are not generally expected to learn the regional languages unless they settle in for a lengthy stay, but they must beware of dismissing them as dialects or of considering their use pretentious. Language is a highly sensitive and politicized issue in Spain, particularly in bilingual areas, and insensitivity can lead to trouble.

Political and Social Changes since 1975

It is impossible to understand modern Spain without some knowledge of the Civil War, the forty-year dictatorship of General Francisco Franco, and the transition to democratic government since General Franco's death in 1975. Spain became a republic in 1931, when the king, Alfonso XIII, "suspended the exercise of royal power" and went into exile (he formally abdicated in 1941). Social and political tensions grew along with economic problems, and the accompanying confrontations between political factions finally erupted with a military uprising in July 1936, led by Franco. This revolt was the beginning of the Civil War that lasted until 1939 and resulted in the defeat of forces loyal to the Republican government by Franco's Nationalists. It is estimated that between one and two million Spaniards died during the war, and massive destruction was inflicted upon the country. Franco became head of state and his dictatorship lasted until his death, when Spain became a monarchy once again under King Juan Carlos, grandson of Alfonso XIII. A series of transitional governments led to the Constitution and elections of 1978. Spain today is a constitutional monarchy with a national parliament and senate in Madrid as well as autonomous regional governments with their own parliaments.

Political feelings run deep in Spain. Some Spaniards who fought in the Civil War are still living. Many Spaniards, including Pablo Picasso, lived out their lives in other countries rather than remain in Spain under Franco. Others stayed in Spain but suffered the consequences of having been on the wrong side in the war. As time passes, the combatants are dying off and a whole new generation exists that was born after the democratic transition. The Civil War and *franquismo* (the Franco era) are now the subject of affectionate memoirs and even comedy. However, Spaniards continue to be politically aware and uncomfortably conscious that their democracy is relatively young and can be threatened.

Foreigners working with Spaniards should be alert to the possibility that their Spanish colleagues may hold radically opposing political views. This is also true in the United States but with three important differences. First, the range of political opinion among Americans is not usually as great, so disagreement may be less extreme. Second, while Americans often separate politics from other activities ("Let's leave politics out of this"), Spaniards often do not. Third, political memories in Spain are longer, so bygones are not bygones.

Spain and Latin America: La Madre Patria

Ties between Spain and Latin America are strong. Columbus made landfall in the Americas in 1492, setting off a wave of Spanish conquest and settlement. Spain imposed its language, laws, architecture, and culture on an empire extending from Florida to Argentina. Many Latin American nations came into being as a result of the wars of independence from

Spain in the early nineteenth century, but it was not until the Spanish-American War of 1898 that Spain lost Puerto Rico and Cuba, its last colonial possessions in the Western Hemisphere.

Diplomatic, governmental and quasi-governmental, commercial, cultural, and emotional ties live on. A flood of Spanish intellectuals found refuge in Mexico after the Spanish Civil War of 1936–39, and in the 1970s Chileans and Argentinians, among others, went to Spain to escape repressive governments at home. A number of Latin American countries allow dual citizenship with Spain. Since 1975 the transition from dictatorship to democracy in Spain has been held up as a model for Latin America. Spain's government is committed to defending the interests of Latin America before those of the European Union in such areas as immigration and trading relationships as well as offering economic and political support for emerging democracies. The term *mother country* seems strange to many Americans, who do not regard England in such a way. But *la madre patria* is a meaningful concept in Spain's relationship with Latin America.

The end of the Cold War has reduced the prospect of Marxist revolution in Latin America, and U.S. foreign policy in the region has become correspondingly less interventionist. At the same time, Spain's economic integration into Europe has been paralleled by the development of the North American Free Trade Agreement (between Canada, the United States, and Mexico) and other free-trade zones such as Mercosur (between Chile and Argentina). With investment money flowing more freely than ever between the United States, Latin America, and Spain, relationships—or at least the tone of the debate—have become more focused on economic development than political ideology.

Many Americans learning Spanish are first exposed to the Latin American variety (known, confusingly, as *castellano*). The difference between this and the Castilian of Spain is comparable to the difference between American and British

English ("I say to-MAY-to and you say to-MAH-to..."). There is a perceptible variation in accent, with the most significant factor being the lisping of *z* and *c* before *e* and *i* in Castilian. This lisp, found in most of Spain, is often the object of mockery in Latin America, while Spaniards tease Argentinians for their characteristic lilting accent and *che* tag—comparable to the Canadian *eh?*—and Mexicans for their use of diminutives—for example, *ahorita* instead of *ahora* (now). But speaking Latin American castellano is not a disability in Spain. One adapts quite quickly to the few significant differences in vocabulary and pronunciation.

Many Americans associate Spanish primarily with Latin America. One American newcomer to Spain, who had learned Spanish in California and visited Mexico, commented, "I can't get used to having these fair-skinned, European-looking people speaking to me in Spanish." Similarly, a common traveler's tale from Spaniards visiting the United States is that identifying yourself as Spanish leads people to assume you are from Latin America. To avoid this, the first thing a Spaniard must say is, "I'm European."

Spain and Europe: Africa Begins at the Pyrenees

Flying to Spain from the north, one passes over the sharp, snow-covered peaks of the Pyrenees. On the other side is Spain. Even from the air, the landscape is unmistakably different. The Pyrenees are the fence between Spain and the rest of Europe, affecting even the weather and giving Spain its famous sunny climate.

"Africa begins at the Pyrenees" is an old saying in Spain, heard less often now as Spain becomes a full-fledged and increasingly respected member of the European Union and NATO. Southern Spain was ruled by Muslims from North Africa for nearly eight hundred years, from the eighth to the fifteenth century. The surrender of the southern kingdom of Granada to the *Reyes Católicos* (Catholic Monarchs) in 1492 finalized the unification of Spain into a single kingdom freed from the Moors. This final conquest, followed by the expulsion later in the year of those Jews and Moors who refused to convert, was a triumph of militant Catholicism. This was the beginning of Spain's so-called Golden Age, which saw the beginning of its empire in the Americas and its rise to power in Europe. However, the expelled Jews and Moors took with them much of the financial, commercial, and agricultural expertise of Spain, sowing the seeds of later economic decline. After 1588 and the defeat of the Spanish Armada, Spain's political power also waned. Increasingly isolated, Spain became embroiled in the Napoleonic Wars and a struggle for independence from France that left behind a hostility to the French that has continued to the present day. Spaniards have had a love-hate relationship with other European countries, especially Spain's political rivals and wartime enemies. During the colonial era England, Holland, and France actively fomented the *leyenda negra* (evil legend) of Spain's backwardness, cruelty, arrogance, and bigotry. Following Spain's defeat in the Spanish-American War, a whole generation of Spanish intellectuals turned critical eyes on the shortcomings of their own country, perpetuating Spain's sense of separateness and isolation. After its Civil War, Spain was isolated again, ostracized by the European and North American democracies and cut off from many of the vital political and social changes that stirred Europe after the Second World War.

During the late 1950s and most of the 1960s large numbers of Spaniards emigrated to Germany and France as guest workers. A rising standard of living in those countries created jobs that their own nationals were unwilling to fill but that were attractive to people from poor farming and fishing villages in Spain. Some of these emigrants stayed, while many others returned to Spain with money they could never have earned at home. The exodus of part of its population to serve as low-paid manual workers in more developed countries did nothing for the Spanish self-image.

In the 1960s "sunny Spain," where the weather was good and prices were low, became the prime vacation spot for northerners. Today, though prices have risen to general European levels, large numbers of Europeans still flock to Spain for vacations, and many own vacation or retirement homes there. As in similar places the world over, these vacationers remain ignorant of Spain, which is a source of irritation to Spaniards.

Somos el vagón de la cola, Spaniards used to say, meaning "We always bring up the rear." Technology, intellectual and social movements, and political changes all seemed to come from the north and reach Spain late, or never. As late as the 1970s, Spaniards would take bus tours to Perpignan in southern France to see movies that had been banned by the Spanish censors because of their political or social content.

In the years since its entry into the European Union in 1986, Spain has somewhat evolved from its old status of "end of the line." The events of 1992 (the Olympic Games in Barcelona, the World's Fair in Seville, and the Columbus quincentennial) brought positive exposure to the "new Spain." With the support of international investors and E.U. development funds, the Spanish economy has raced to catch up with the rest of Europe and has produced some of the highest growth rates on the continent.

On the political front, prominent Spaniards have made the step into E.U. politics, and Spaniards are active at all levels of the E.U. administration. Greater visibility and prestige have also accrued from Spain's turn in the presidency of the E.U. (which rotates to a different member each year) and from international peace conferences held in Madrid. Paralleling these developments, Spanish music, theater, literature, cinema, and art have found expanded audiences all over Europe.

These developments, particularly on the political and economic front, are a source of pride for Spaniards. For better or worse, Spain is now a developed European country rather than just a backward, "sun and cheap wine" vacation spot.

Spain and the United States

Historical Relationship

In 1985 the state of Texas celebrated the 150th anniversary of its independence from Mexico. Like Florida, New Mexico, Arizona, and California, Texas had been a part of the Spanish empire. During the early 1800s that empire began to break up, and in 1898 Spain's last New World territories were lost with the end of the Spanish-American War.

In 1936, with the outbreak of the Spanish Civil War, the United States once again became closely involved with events in Spain. The government of the Republic called for help, which was provided by the International Brigades recruited in various countries, including the United States.

The Franco government was diplomatically isolated by the United States until the 1950s, when it was formally recognized; in 1953 Spain and the United States signed a mutual defense and aid treaty. Under this treaty one U.S. naval base and three U.S. air bases were established in various parts of Spain, with about twelve thousand U.S. military personnel.

The issue of the bases was tied in with Spain's membership in NATO (OTAN in Spanish). The delicacy of the issue and the multiplicity of views and attitudes in relation to it are exemplified by the Spanish Socialist party. As an opposition party, Socialist leaders were firmly opposed to NATO membership and promised a referendum on the issue if elected. When they came to power, however, while they did call the referendum, they also executed a 180-degree turn on the issue and advocated continued membership. The result of the referendum was a narrow margin in favor of NATO. One of the most common graffiti in Spain used to be *OTAN No—Bases Fuera* (No to NATO—Out with the bases). Those who opposed NATO and the U.S. military bases felt that they involved Spain in the consequences of events that Spain did not determine or control. The U.S. bombing of Tripoli, Libya, in 1986 caused an angry reaction among many Spaniards, who felt that they were in the direct line of fire for reprisals while Americans were safely ensconced on the other side of the Atlantic.

When, in contrast to the surprise bombing of Tripoli, President George Bush in 1990 sought an international coalition against Iraq after its invasion of Kuwait, Spain lent its support, as it did in later years to peacekeeping operations in Bosnia. In the 1990s Spain's successful transition to democracy and the end of the Cold War caused the United States to downsize its military presence in Spain. In 1996 former Spanish Foreign Minister Javier Solana was the first Spaniard to be appointed head of NATO, now a more European organization focusing on the promises and threats of the former Communist bloc. In its relationship with the United States, Spain is now part of a relatively prosperous and powerful Europe, rather than a poor country cousin.

As statesmen love to say, relationships between countries are about people as much as governments. On an individual level, the political relationship between Spain and the United States has led to miscommunication and misunderstanding. A main cause of such problems is the relative level of knowledge Spaniards and Americans have about international politics.

In the United States, events on the international scene are presented by the mainstream media in a sporadic fashion, often based on crisis or folklore. An event that is perceived as significant (such as an election or assassination) in a foreign country is headline news for a brief period; then media interest evaporates. Local newspapers or network television give brief "human interest" coverage to quaint foreign customs—in the case of Spain, the annual running of the bulls in Pamplona or *El gordo* Christmas lottery (The Big One). A minority of Americans are both interested and knowledgeable and stay current through national newspapers and the Internet, but most Americans have little understanding of the international scene, and particularly U.S. impact on it.

They usually think of the U.S. role in world leadership and
the American troops deployed around the globe as a sign of
generosity and commitment to preserving democracy. Not
many Americans accept that the U.S. role is not always
positive.

Spaniards watching the evening news on their local television stations or reading their local newspapers are exposed
to daily coverage of international events. Because of the
strategic position of the United States in world affairs, this
coverage includes American international policies and domestic politics. The attitude of the media varies, with some
programs, newspapers, or magazines more pro-American than
others. Throughout, there is intense interest, detailed analysis, and sometimes scathing criticism of American politics
and society.

Anti-American sentiment exists, especially among Spaniards who became adults in the 1960s and who passed through
Spanish universities at that time. This is not to say that
Americans can expect open hostility, but rather that they
may find among the people they meet distinct reservations
about U.S. policies. Generally speaking, the more left-wing
the source, the stronger the disapproval of American policies
and the more the United States is likely to be seen as an
intruder or aggressor rather than as a friendly protector.

Americans are surprised, and often resentful, at Spanish
interest in and judgments of the United States. Most Americans believe that the U.S. system of democracy is an example
for the world. They may be aware of declining voter turnout
and the turf battles and deal making that characterize the
messy reality of politics at the federal, state, and local levels;
however, this does not sully their belief in democracy, because of two characteristics of the American system. One is
idealism: the belief that individuals and societies can and
should be made better through effort. The other is the rule of
law, the system of checks and balances, and the accountability of elected officials and public servants. The situation in

Spain is different on both counts. First, rather than idealistic, Spaniards are generally cynical, professing a gloomy pessimism that may not always correspond to their true feelings. Second, accountability and the rule of law were casualties of the totalitarian past, and their reinstatement is one of the hardest tasks of the democratic transition.

Politics in Spain and the United States are relatively similar in general, but there are differences. Spain's Civil War is far more recent, and its shadow is longer because of the nearly forty years of the Franco dictatorship. Political thinking is more polarized, though less so than a generation ago. Political violence is more organized and widespread than in the U.S. As for the American political scene, the presidential election process (including party congresses), the presence of the religious right, and recurrent public moralizing by political figures are more colorful than in Spain.

Unless they have closely studied or personally experienced the American scene, Spaniards do not understand the influence of U.S. domestic politics on U.S. foreign policy. If they disagree with a foreign policy position taken by the U.S. president, they are likely to say so to the nearest American.

Americans may feel personally attacked when Spaniards question them in what seems to be an aggressive way about U.S. policies toward the rest of the world. Feeling attacked, they may strike back: angry Americans may be skeptical of Spanish democracy, quick to find fault with Spanish politics, and scornful of Spaniards for submitting to forty years of the Franco dictatorship.

There is another way. Americans who do not wish to discuss politics, especially when they feel obliged to be advocates of or apologists for their country's policies, can simply change the subject as politely as possible. Spaniards are generally courteous enough not to pursue the discussion. Also, Americans should remember that it is quite possible for a Spaniard to be anti-American politically and yet pro-American personally.

14

Images

Images of the United States permeate the media of other countries to an extent that most Americans do not realize. American TV series are sold around the world, as are American products, and both have an enormous influence in conditioning what people think about Americans.

One image Spaniards hold of the United States is that of the "Wild West." They see the Marlboro man on billboards and in magazines. Generations of TV shows in Western settings have captured the imagination of Spaniards and live on in reruns. Everyone knows from TV and movies that real people still walk around wearing cowboy boots and ten-gallon hats, even if they have never been near a horse in their lives.

Another image is that of the Elvis era: the fifties, with huge cars, full skirts and bobby sox, and rock and roll. The appeal of this era is that it corresponds to a time when young people in Spain were much less liberated than they are today and looked to the United States (as represented in American movies) as the symbol of a freedom they did not have.

Gangsters and their modern-day counterparts are a vital feature of Spain's image of the United States. Al Capone captured the imagination of Spain through movies. Even the word *gangster* has been adopted into Spanish, and the Spanish words *ganster* and *gansterismo* refer to lawlessness and organized street crime. Spaniards believe the United States to be a dangerous country; they think of the streets of American cities as pitched battlefields with shoot-outs on every corner. Reports of organized crime, drug-related and gang violence, and "action" movies serve only to confirm the gangster image. Cities with skyscrapers, freeways, corners lending themselves to ambushes, and streets designed for car chases are the stuff of so many crime-fighter TV shows and movies that many Spaniards do not realize there is anything else to American life. (Spaniards, used to densely crowded cities with endemic parking problems, find it hard to believe that heroes and villains alike can always find a parking place whenever and wherever they need one.)

Because most Spanish visitors to the United States seldom venture beyond the major cities, their image of the United States is that of a vast urban sprawl. Their first destination is usually New York, followed by Florida, where they visit Disney World and Miami. Chicago, San Francisco, and Los Angeles are other popular destinations. Rarely do tourists visit a small town or the countryside.

American movies and TV shows project an image of wealth. Movies that deal with poverty in the United States are restricted to the art movie circuit and do not usually reach general audiences. Spaniards are aware of poverty in the United States from newspaper articles, but this information does not offset the impression created by lush TV and movie sets.

Spaniards imagine Americans to be uncultured and unaware of anything outside their own limited experience. This myth has undoubtedly been reinforced by Americans who arrive in Europe without a shred of information about the countries where they will be living. One Spaniard told a story of an American woman he met in New York in a professional capacity. In the course of conversation she inquired, "You have a king in Europe, don't you?" Further contributing to the image of boorish Americans is the American style of doing business. The habit of going straight to the point in meetings and negotiations rather than indulging in some preliminary get-acquainted, personal conversation makes a negative impression on Spaniards, who think Americans must have nothing else to talk about.

Americans' images of Spain are often rather confused. Some may have seen *El Cid* or *Man of La Mancha*, which present images of medieval exoticism in the midst of poverty and arid landscapes. Others know Spain as the images from Pedro Almodóvar's movies, which present a modern urban landscape that is slightly surreal.

Americans confuse Spain with Latin America and therefore think of Spaniards as swarthy, Indian-looking individuals, perpetually engaged in civil wars and revolutions against
dictatorships. So enduring is this confusion that tourists in
Spain regularly buy huge Mexican-style sombreros, complete
with pointed tops and tasseled brims. No Spaniard wears or
has ever worn such a hat, though they do produce them for
sale to tourists.

When Spain began to promote tourism during the 1960s,
much was made of the most exotic and salable traditions:
bullfighting, flamenco dancing, and ladies in frilly skirts sitting on horseback behind Latin Lovers in tight dark suits.
These images still persist among Americans, to the dismay of
many Spaniards. Bullfighting in Spain is like hunting in the
United States—it exists and has enthusiastic supporters but
also many opponents. Nothing in Ernest Hemingway's writ-
ings on Spain, read by generations of Americans, suggests
that Spaniards are ambivalent about bullfighting. Similarly,
many Spaniards have no idea how to do any kind of Spanish
dancing; and the costume of frilly skirts and polka dots is
restricted to special occasions in Andalucía.

Finally, Spain has a "fun in the sun" image that was also
projected as part of the tourist campaign of the 1960s and
ensuing years. Sun, beaches, wine, and fiestas were the bait
set to catch tourists. Countless people have visited Spain and
gone no further than some beach resort, where they can
function in their own language and eat familiar food. While
this is more typical of English and German visitors, lots of
Americans have also visited Spain and come away with
memories only of good food, late nights, singing and dancing,
and relaxing on the beach. They remember Spain only as a
place where people lack many of the American conveniences
of life but know how to have fun and enjoy good food and
wine. The quintessential vacation spot is Marbella, the luxury
resort on the south coast, where the world's dandies and
millionaires go to spend their leisure time, moving from ex-

clusive club to extravagant party or luxury fashion show and assiduously encouraging the gossip magazines of Spain and elsewhere to keep their names in circulation.

Spaniards, like other Europeans, have ambivalent feelings about American popular culture. They are distressed by the influx of American fast-food chains, pop music, and television programs (teenagers, of course, are delighted). While no educated Spaniard would admit to taking popular TV shows as a true picture of American life, the programs do project an image of the United States that many Spaniards love to hate.

Nevertheless, admiration for the United States is widespread, although it often coexists with resentment. Scholars, artists, exchange students, researchers, and businesspeople visit the States in large numbers every year, and many Spaniards now holding high positions once studied there. A visit to New York and California is the dream of many young people, and most of those who have been to the United States have fond memories of their experience.

Technology

Spaniards regard the United States as a source of know-how and technical expertise, an exporter of skills and technology to other countries. Spaniards generally have a lot of admiration for American technology—in the "hard" sense of machines, techniques, and products—as well as the "soft" side of technology, which is the approach and way of doing things. System, details, and the handbook approach—writing everything down so that things can be done consistently in the most efficient way—are seen by Spaniards as being typically American.

Spaniards are usually willing to concede to Americans on the technical front, but Americans often have a hard time distinguishing between teaching Spaniards techniques and processes and teaching them the American way of doing things. For instance, one Spanish executive at a corporate training seminar was criticized for his speaking manner. The

American seminar leader, fresh from the New York home office, found the Spaniard's oral presentations too diffuse. He tried to instill the point-by-point approach basic to American public speaking: tell them what you're going to say; say it; then tell them what you've said. The Spaniard resisted this speaking style, claiming that it was alien both to him and to his Spanish clients.

Americans often feel irritated at being brought to Spain to demonstrate something only to meet resistance from Spaniards. However, such resistance is inevitable if the American is trying to show Spaniards how to be like Americans. Most Spaniards do not wish to be like Americans; they only want to have the benefit of their know-how. Therefore, to be successful in Spain, Americans must be able to sift out technique from attitude.

While Americans are (according to Spaniards) relatively lacking in personal arrogance, they have an ingrained conviction of the superiority of things American. They tend to distrust Spanish products, from cars to home appliances, and assume that they are poorly made and unrepairable. There are Spanish products, especially imitations of American products, that *are* inferior: for example, imitation Post-it notes that stick for only a minute and then ignominiously fall off. However, the undifferentiated assumption by Americans that everything Spanish will be shoddy is inaccurate. In fact the quality of Spanish consumer products is steadily improving, because of increased buying power and the influence of European standards. For their part, Spaniards note how many American products are actually manufactured offshore. Many Spaniards also take pride in their preference for good-quality items that they maintain and repair, rather than the cheap throwaways fostered by American consumer culture.

Americans arriving in Spain should realize that they will be seen both as individuals and as symbols. As individuals they will be taken on their own merits. But they should not be startled if a taxi driver passes judgment on the last American presidential election or a friend takes them to task about U.S. foreign policy.

Adaptation

The principal lesson that Americans can learn from their experience in any other country lies in the area of cultural relativity. They learn that not only do people in other cultures do things differently, but they prefer to do them that way. Americans sometimes criticize the very things Spaniards are most proud of, such as their casual attitude toward rules and regulations. Or Spaniards may agree with Americans about a particular behavior such as their lack of punctuality but still prefer the Spanish value orientation to, in this case, time.

One would not have to look far to find countries and cultures that are more alien to the United States than Spain, which is, after all, a part of Western Europe, with a history that is closely linked to that of the U.S. and a worldview and social organization that are recognizably similar. Spaniards prize democracy and the rights of the individual. Spain's sense of its international role parallels that of the United States.

Spaniards, like Americans, are proud of their achievements and have comparable ambitions and aspirations. Spaniards and Americans alike take pleasure in friends and family and enjoy sports, movies, books, and music. On the cultural, educational, and political levels, enough cross-pollination has taken place for many things to be familiar.

Yet the differences between Americans and Spaniards cause friction. Different concepts of time or different negotiating styles may be a curiosity or an irritation. What turns them into real stumbling blocks is when one or the other of the parties refuses to accept a different way just because it is different. Such intolerance and inflexibility lead to trouble.

So do hasty and oversimplified judgments, which, if based on hearsay or media images, are perhaps even more annoying than if based on personal impressions. Whatever the source, these judgments are insulting and usually resented.

It seems that in situations of conflict both Spaniards and Americans become "more so." If pushed, Americans become more rule-bound, stuffy, and priggish (as Spaniards see it). Meanwhile, Spaniards become more defiant, emotional, and irrational (according to Americans).

It may seem unfair to American readers that much of the emphasis of this book is on how they can best adapt to Spain and to Spaniards. This reaction is understandable, especially since many Spaniards are no more adept at tolerating differences than are Americans. This point is made nicely by Fernando Diaz-Plaja in *The Spaniard and the Seven Deadly Sins*, his lighthearted yet scholarly portrait of his own people:

> The way to improve the Spaniard can be summed up in a possibility as simple as it is revolutionary.
>
> If from time to time, only from time to time, we were to believe that the other man might be right...
>
> And if this belief did not automatically make him odious...
>
> I believe that would be enough.[1]

At any rate, the outsider is the one who has to do most of the adapting, but Spaniards are traditionally tolerant, welcoming, and often admiring of foreigners and their funny ways. Furthermore, Spaniards take adaptation to Spain as a compliment. They are pleased when foreigners know Spanish, take an interest in customs and traditions, and travel around and get to know the country.

---

[1] Fernando Diaz-Plaja, *The Spaniard and the Seven Deadly Sins* (London: Pan Books, 1971), 211. Originally published in Spanish as *El español y los siete pecados capitales*. Madrid: Alianza Editorial, 1966.

Encounter One: Maleducado

Jeff is a professor on a Fulbright scholarship, teaching American literature at a Spanish university. Accustomed to a small private college, he dislikes the crowded, smoky, noisy halls of the university and usually hurries to and from his office as quickly and unobtrusively as possible, speaking to no one. He knew no Spanish prior to coming to Spain, and though he is taking Spanish classes, he does not find the language easy—another reason why he feels shy around groups of Spaniards talking loudly at high speed.

One day Jeff buys a bottle of wine to take to dinner at a friend's house after work and accidentally drops it on the tiled floor of his office. Broken glass flies everywhere and a pool of wine covers the floor. Jeff goes looking for one of the housekeepers to ask her to come and clean up. She is slow to understand what he wants, answers abruptly, and keeps him waiting in his office for quite some time before she arrives with her mop and broom. Why?

> *Over time, Jeff has unwittingly offended many people, including the maintenance staff, by hastening past them without a greeting. He has been labeled a rude (maleducado) and standoffish person. Based on this reputation, the housekeeper is unwilling to help him.*

COMMENT: As in many countries where wine is abundant and apparently omnipresent, its use is strictly regulated by custom and convention. A university professor's office is not the place for a bottle of wine. Further, Spaniards have seen enough drunk tourists and alcoholic expatriates to have developed some stereotypes about foreigners and wine. Disapproval on this score may also have influenced the housekeeper's attitude.

2

Society and the Individual

Any attempt to describe culture brings with it the danger of overgeneralization and stereotyping. Individual Americans or Spaniards may feel that they are not accurately described in the analyses that follow. The intent is not to deny individuality but rather to describe cultural differences.

Americans and Spaniards differ markedly in their beliefs regarding the importance of individualism and how the individual fits into society. The most visible differences are often superficial, but those that are less visible are often the most fundamental and can cause misunderstanding or friction.

Family

A major difference that Americans notice is the close-knit family structure in Spain. Extended families usually live in the same city, often in the same neighborhood, and sometimes in the same building. Family members frequently work together in family businesses, and grandparents commonly take care of babies and small children while mothers are out at work. Lunch on Sundays and holidays is a ritual involving the entire extended family. Spanish young people generally live at home until their midtwenties or until they marry. This is very different from the United States, where the expectation is that children will leave home by the end of their teens and will delay departure or come back to live only if forced to do so by a limited job market, high housing costs, or a personal crisis.

Americans often wonder if this closeness with family doesn't stifle individuality in Spaniards, producing people who follow custom and tradition without question. Spaniards, on the other hand, often see Americans as rootless, cast out of the home too young and forced to make their own way without the benefit of financial and moral support and a network of family contacts.

Perhaps the fundamental difference between Spanish and American individualism is that for an American, personal individuality or independence is a state of mind and source of identity as well as a lifestyle. For Americans, the Spanish way, which seems to subordinate individuality to social appearances and family loyalty, must result in a loss of personal identity. Spaniards, however, don't see it that way.

For Spaniards, the extended family constitutes a social and economic support system. Spaniards typically start dating their future spouses in high school or, at the latest, university and marry in their mid- or late twenties; there is a long period of courtship during which each of the partners becomes almost as closely integrated into the spouse's family—the *familia política,* or in-laws—as into his or her own. The result is a dual support system, the significance of which is captured in a wry Spanish proverb: *Vive de tus padres hasta que puedas vivir de tus hijos* (Live off your parents until you can live off your children). To an outsider, it may seem that this is really what Spaniards do. If one's parents have money, it is as good as having it oneself. Americans too can expect to inherit from their parents, but in most cases they do not consider their future inheritance as affecting the amount of money they can and should earn today. However, many Spaniards generally have routine access to family money. Young people will say,

"I have an apartment at the seaside" or "I have a cottage in the country," when in fact the property is owned by the parents. It belongs to the family and, therefore, to each member.

Many adult Americans maintain close ties to their immediate family (parents and siblings), but few are involved with their extended family to the extent that is typical with Spaniards. This is partly because the size of the United States and the mobility of individuals mean that many Americans only see their extended family at occasional reunions. Those Spaniards who have moved away from their hometown or village for work or study typically return for at least a part of every annual vacation. Spaniards don't have American-style family reunions.

Extended family support permeates Spanish professional as well as personal life. As noted earlier, many people work in family businesses, and even in the wider work environment family ties still count. People will try to help other members of their extended family find employment in the company where they work or another company where they have influence. The central importance of personal contacts, which will be discussed in more detail later, starts with the family. Relatives and in-laws routinely help out younger members of the family; this tradition is becoming, if anything, stronger as high levels of unemployment in Spain persist and work is difficult to find.

Given these circumstances, the foreigner should not be surprised to find that a Spanish colleague's professional network includes many family members and reaches out into the extended family to include cousins, godparents, and in-laws. While most Spanish employees do not have photographs of their spouse and children on their desks, family members probably impinge more on working life than the smiling figures pictured on the American's desk.

Most national *convenios*, or job agreements, give employees the right to paid days off for family emergencies such as severe illness or death of a family member. There is a short period (several days) of paid paternity leave for men whose wives have just had a baby. The 1993 Family and Medical Leave Act provides parental or health-related leave for some U.S. workers, but such leave is unpaid, while a three-month paid maternity leave is the legal norm in Spain. A Spaniard who goes into the hospital can expect to have family there for every minute of visiting hours. Private clinics, which allow visitors round the clock, even provide beds for family members in the patient's room, since someone will be there day and night. Female employees with children under school age are entitled to leave work an hour earlier each day. And most husbands will take time off work to accompany their pregnant wives on routine visits to the doctor.

The link between the family network and professional life in Spain is something many Americans vaguely disapprove of. It seems to smack of nepotism and other concepts alien to the American ideal of self-reliance and independence. Naturally, there are cases of incompetents who have obtained, through *enchufe* (contacts), positions they do not deserve. However, in most cases the existence of connections creates a relationship of loyalty and obligation that can enhance an employee's value.

Spaniards, for their part, generally have mixed feelings about American family style. They think desktop photographs of family are cute but odd. As for the American habit of moving to the other side of the country or the world without a backward glance, most Spaniards are both envious and dismayed. They can see the benefits of not being encumbered by the relationships involved in a close family network, but they can also see the disadvantages of doing without the support the family network provides. Most Spaniards would probably say, "It's all right for them, but it wouldn't do for me."

Spaniards assume that families will stay close despite disagreements. They expect differences to be downplayed rather than becoming divisive; estrangement from family members is to be avoided. This may seem hypocritical to Americans, who tend to prefer disclosure to concealment and hold individual beliefs to be more important than any greater loyalty, sometimes even including family. Nonetheless, Americans should hesitate before discussing personal matters, especially problems. Spaniards disclose such things only to family and intimate friends. Workmates may fall into this category, since many Spaniards work so long in the same company that their workmates become another "family," but the American is by definition a temporary visitor. Spaniards will feel uncomfortable hearing about the personal problems of an American they don't know well.

Serious trouble can arise in American-Spanish marriages when it comes to raising children. The American is invariably stricter than the Spaniard about mealtimes, snacks, treats, and naps. Spanish children typically enjoy large quantities of attention and few rules at home.

Americans are amazed to see children out and about with their parents at midnight, perceiving this as an example of overindulgence. In fact, the children are up late not because they ask to be but because they have no choice. Spanish children are expected to participate without complaining in many adult activities such as shopping and eating out. Spanish parents are fairly strict with their children in public, chastising them verbally or even physically for misbehavior or impoliteness. In this sense, they are not indulged at all.

As they grow older, Spanish children are likely to feel more academic pressure than Americans, with rigorous school curricula, extra lessons, and lots of homework. Spanish teenagers spending a junior year in American high schools are amazed at the relatively light load of schoolwork. On the other hand, American parents in Spain may miss the opportunities for clubs, sporting activities, and paid work that they see as rounding out the teenage experience.

Groups and Communities

Class

Egalitarianism is one of the most cherished American ideals. Many Americans will affirm that the United States is a class-less society, while Europe is straitjacketed by class consciousness. The "rags to riches" ideal of a person who can start off as nobody and rise to wealth and power, as many have done in the U.S., is difficult to imagine in Europe. The ongoing influence in the U.S. of European immigrants in search of a better life and more opportunity has contributed to a belief among many Americans that social systems in Europe are unjust and even feudal. It sometimes seems that Americans who come to Spain are looking for confirmation of this belief and are predisposed to find signs of rigid class structures. They latch on gleefully to the idea of enchufe, for instance, as proof that in Spain, unlike the U.S., "It's not what you know, but who you know." At the same time many U.S. companies trying to establish themselves in Spain want to make use of upper-class networks of money and influence, and they set out to recruit at least some of their top executives from socially prominent families. This may lead to a kind of confused schizophrenia in top American managers based in Spain.

In Spain, social classes are clearly defined and are strongly influenced by historical developments. During the reconquest of Spain from the Muslims, the society underwent a process of social reorganization and re-Christianization. Social status came from being an "old Christian," not a convert. It also meant being pure-blooded, without Moorish or Jewish ancestry. In many parts of Spain a gentleman, in addition to being an old Christian with pure blood, was also someone who had never worked for his living, but who fought in the reconquest and was rewarded with lands off which he then lived. To be upper class in Spain in those days meant a life of idleness and attitudes of religious intolerance and racial exclusiveness. This is a far cry from the American ideal in which status is achieved through hard work, the result of which is the accumulation of money and social influence.

What residue of the fifteenth century still remains in Spanish society? Much and little. Everyone in Spain is officially Catholic, though in fact there are synagogues, mosques, and a constellation of Protestant churches; and the percentage of the population that goes to church regularly is smaller in Spain than in the United States (a fact which comes as a shock to many Americans). The right wing of Spanish politics is fiercely Catholic and openly antisemitic, anti-Muslim, and racist. There are still huge estates owned by individuals and worked by tenant farmers, especially in Andalucía. The aristocracy is alive and well, and every day even *El País*, an independent newspaper that is distinctly left of center, carries on its society page announcements of aristocratic titles that have been inherited, reinstated, or solicited. In the phrase of one American commentator, the jet set of Madrid is "studded with dukes and playboys." However, an educated, middle-class meritocracy has been clearly on the rise for some years.

An important relic of the high status of idleness is the denigration of manual labor. "Do-it-yourself" is on the increase, but mainly because the cost of home repairs and redecoration has risen steeply. Very few Spaniards would show the kind of pride in a manual job well done that leads Americans to display their handiwork (painting, carpentry, gardening) to visitors.

Another significant fact is that in Spain people do not do work that crosses class lines. It would be unheard-of for a person from the middle class to take such jobs as delivering newspapers or waiting tables, which are part of growing up in middle-class America. Many university students work, but in teaching or white-collar jobs. Class distinctions are perpetuated through this equation of jobs to social status. In the United States, while employment and social status are related, there is also the belief that any job is better than none if you need the money. Such pragmatism is very American; a Spaniard would feel that, with family to help, one should never need the money so badly as to be willing to take a low-status job.

In Spanish corporations, the higher echelons are still filled to a great extent by the upper class. Even though there is now a rising generation of middle-class professionals, members of the moneyed upper classes have traditionally had better opportunities. At a time when English was still not widely taught in the public schools, children of the Spanish well-to-do had English tutors and were sent to summer camp in England or Ireland for the finishing touches. From private schools they moved on to private institutes for further education. At these schools they associated with their social peers and established the contacts that then led to internships in international companies, work experience in the United States, and so on. These are the people that American companies tend to hire, both because their qualifications are superior and because their social position ensures that they have good contacts with the world of money and influence. Top executives and, to a certain extent, executive secretaries are from the upper classes. The rude slang word for them in Spanish is *pijos*, meaning spoiled rich kids. By tradition and experience, they are often pro-American, which is another factor that makes them desirable to American companies. In dealing with upper-class coworkers, however, an American manager may be shocked at some of the attitudes they express, especially those that betray racial, religious, and class prejudices that an American would hesitate to express publicly because they go so much against the grain of the egalitarian American ideal and are illegal. Furthermore, the attitudes of these people tend to vary substantially from those of the solid middle class who make up the bulk of the Spanish white-collar employees.

Minorities and Immigrants

In comparison with American society, Spain has a low level of racial diversity; in fact, it is one of the most homogeneous societies in Europe. Until recently Spain's most significant minority group was the Rom (Romany or Gypsies). Easily identifiable by their appearance—dark complexions, black-clad men, women wearing petticoats and large gold earrings—Rom people lived segregated lives, working as market vendors and petty traders and dwelling in shantytowns or moving from place to place. Gypsies were stereotyped as aliens, beggars, and petty criminals; limited access to health care and education perpetuated their outcast status. Only in Andalucía did they find some degree of acceptance because of their strong influence on flamenco music. Although this picture of the Gypsies is recognizable today, Rom representatives have successfully lobbied the European Union for improvements in their rights and status. Spain is implementing a Gypsy Development Program to redress the situation brought about by centuries of segregation.

As for immigrant minorities, Spain's experience has differed from that of its northern neighbors. Spain had neither African and Asian colonial possessions nor the post-World War II boom that attracted Third-World immigrants to northern European countries such as France, Britain, and Germany. Rather, Spaniards emigrated to more developed northern economies. The only exception to this were the former Spanish territories in North Africa, which were and continue to be the largest source of non-European immigrants to Spain. Immigrants also come from Latin America and, more recently, sub-Saharan Africa, but never in the large numbers seen in northern countries. Immigrant people of color, working as domestics and agricultural laborers, form a tiny minority of Spanish society. Posing no threat to the status quo, they tend to be treated tolerantly. In recent years, however, Spain has tightened its formerly lax immigration and naturalization policies under pressure from the European Union.

City and Neighborhood

An American woman, recently arrived in Barcelona, was staying with her Spanish boyfriend in the area of the city that is said to equal Calcutta in population density and lack of open spaces. Low-cost high-rise apartment buildings line a road that is one of the highway accesses to Barcelona, with all the attendant noise and pollution. After a few days, the woman said, "I want to see where the rich people live." Accordingly, her friend took her to the "upper zone," as it is called. The streets were quieter and the apartment buildings were handsome and surrounded by small patches of lawn or shrubbery. There was usually a *portero*, or doorman, who monitored visitors and kept everything in order. "But," said the American despairingly, "they're still apartments."

Indeed, Spanish city dwellers live in apartments. Many own a chalet in the countryside or an apartment at the beach, to which they retire for weekends and vacations. But suburbs, with separate homes surrounded by their own yards, are restricted to a few modern developments (*urbanizaciónes*) around the big cities. Because of this great physical difference between Spanish and American cities, Americans often have a hard time perceiving that Spanish cities also have neighborhoods. That is to say, each city has not only its old and new areas, its rich, middle-income, and decayed zones—as do most North American and European cities—but also specific and very clearly defined neighborhoods, not more than a few blocks square, that are little communities with stable populations. They are in fact like villages within the city, and it is common for people to live all their lives in one such "village." Of course, this is not true of everyone. Some people move from one part of the city to another to be nearer their work or their families, and a few move out of the city to an urbanización. Huge old apartments in the city centers are now being bought and restored by well-to-do professionals. Nonetheless, the majority of people think of themselves as living in a particular neighborhood.

The idea of neighborhoods in Spanish cities is particularly surprising to Americans because Spaniards do not seem to be neighborly in the American sense. People do not go to one another's homes, but rather meet in the local café. It is most unusual for neighbors to drop in on one another except to discuss a mutual problem, such as a leaky pipe. Further, apartment dwelling in large American cities tends to be impersonal, and those living in apartments know little or nothing about the people living around them. Because of these factors, Americans living in apartments in Spain don't think of themselves as having (or being) neighbors. But the Spanish do regard one another as such. In fact they probably know everything there is to know about one another, especially if there is a portero or portera, whose main, though not official, function is to keep tabs on everyone and pass on gossip. One can be sure that the arrival of anyone new is noted and commented upon, especially when that new person is a foreigner.

Americans living in a Spanish apartment building should accordingly make a point of greeting people they meet in the elevator or in the lobby or when shopping at local stores and markets (which they should do even though driving halfway across the city to a big "hypermarket" may be more familiar and easier to deal with). Becoming part of the neighborhood will help Americans more quickly feel at home.

Spanish ID cards and many official forms carry the phrase *natural de...* (native of...), which refers to the city, town, or village of one's birth. Most Spaniards are still living in their hometowns, though there are people who have moved from one part of the country to another for professional or economic reasons. In particular, people from small towns or villages moved into the big cities in large numbers in the 1950s and early 1960s. However, mobility is far less common than in the United States. The propensity of Americans for moving from one place to another is a source of wonder to many Spaniards. What particularly strikes Spaniards is that

34

when American are asked where they are from, the answer is
the name of the current place of residence. For example, an
American says, "Well, I'm from Minneapolis, though I was
born in Chicago." A Spaniard, on the other hand, will answer, "I'm from Zaragoza, though I've been living in Madrid
for twenty-five years" because of a much stronger sense of
identification with his or her native city.

Much is said about the traditional rivalry between Madrid
(capital of Spain) and Barcelona (capital of Catalonia), and
it does exist, but it is not peculiar to these two cities. Because
Spaniards tend to identify strongly with their hometowns,
rivalry and competition between different cities is common,
a surprise to many Americans. Regional identity is often an
undercurrent in debates about the virtues and shortcomings
of different cities. This type of competition is something that
Americans usually find hard to take seriously, but they can
make it work to their advantage. Spaniards, being proud of
their cities, are always happy to show them off or to advise
newcomers on places to go or things to see. By getting to
know the city, Americans will feel more at home themselves
and will also win the goodwill of Spanish acquaintances, thus
easing the process of settling in.

Attitudes toward Authority

Citizenship
Spaniards are notoriously indifferent to the needs of others.
Despite their strong sense of community, Spaniards describe
themselves as *insolidarios* (lacking in solidarity). The idea of
good citizenship, which in Spanish is called *civismo*, is something that most Spaniards associate wistfully with other countries. Many trivial irritations experienced by Americans living in Spain derive from this lack of civismo and inability to
attribute importance to the needs or rights of others.

Littering is one example. The streets and sidewalks of
Spanish cities are strewn with scraps of paper and cigarette

butts. It is safe to say that a Spaniard's first instinct in dispos-
ing of an unwanted item is to throw it on the ground. One
American mother in Spain told of buying a cupcake for her
child in a bakery. There was no wastebasket visible, so the
mother told the child to put the paper wrapper on the counter.
The woman behind the counter good-naturedly scolded the
child for putting rubbish on the counter. "Throw it on the
floor!" she said. In Spanish cafés and bars, all the wastepaper
and crumbs from the counter are routinely swept onto the
floor, creating a mess that is not cleaned up until closing time
and that has dissuaded more than one foreigner from ventur-
ing in.

Fernando Diaz-Plaja, in *The Spaniard and the Seven Deadly
Sins*,[1] graphically describes the way Spaniards arriving late
for a movie will make a noise, talk loudly to one another, and
generally act oblivious to the fact that they are disturbing
other, more punctual moviegoers who are trying to watch the
film. American teachers in Spain have found that at exam
time students who hand in their papers early and leave the
room almost always stand just outside discussing the test in
loud voices, without taking into consideration that they might
be impeding the concentration of those still taking the exam.

The majority of bars, discotheques, and restaurants in Spain
are in regular storefront premises, with several stories of apartments above. Most of these places of entertainment post a
rather pathetic sign on the front door saying *Respeten el
descanso de los vecinos* (Respect the sleep of our neighbors), in
the hope of discouraging people who leave in the small hours
of the morning from whooping it up, which of course the
departing patrons do anyway.

The mistake that Americans often make is to think that
inconsiderate behavior is deliberate or malicious in intent.
Nothing could be further from the truth. In all these in-
stances, if asked to stop making the noise, Spaniards will
invariably apologize and do their best to keep their voices
down. The initial irritant, however, is there: Spaniards do

not think about other people until the fact that they are annoying them is called to their attention. What happens most commonly is that Americans, expecting Spaniards to be more considerate, assume that by being noisy or otherwise insolidarios, Spaniards are deliberately trying to be offensive. The typical response of Americans is to suffer in resentful silence, suppressing their feelings until things become intolerable, and then to react angrily. Spaniards, usually amazed by the vehemence with which Americans vent their feelings, say soothingly, *"¿Haberlo dicho, hombre?"* ("Why didn't you say something before?"). This usually does not mollify Americans, because what they are really objecting to is not so much the behavior as the attitudes behind it. If they are sufficiently irritated to start criticizing the manners of the Spaniards, then real trouble is likely to follow, since any accusation of having bad manners or being boorish (maleducado) is an insult in Spain. Unfortunately, maleducado is frequently the word Americans choose to describe someone who is simply being undisciplined in the American sense.

The Individual and the Law

Americans are taught to believe in a government of, for, and by the people. Institutions and officials are held accountable to the public. To outsiders, Americans seem very much aware of the law: both their obligation to abide by it and their right to bring about change when the law seems unreasonable. Americans think it normal to join interest groups and contact elected officials at the city, state, and national level on any issue they deem important.

For much of Spain's history, laws were arbitrarily imposed from above. There was no social contract balancing the responsibilities of rulers and the ruled. Most citizens felt that no benefits would accrue from complying with the law; since enforcement was uncertain, they might get away with flouting it, and there was certainly no way to change it. Though the will of the people was expressed through regional *cortes* (parliaments), these bodies were easily disregarded or over-ruled by the monarch.

The people's defense was to ignore the law if they could and comply only if they must. In the Spanish colonies of the Americas, there was a phrase often used by the servants of the Spanish crown: Obedezco, pero no cumplo (I obey but do not comply). Regulations that were seen as inappropriate were not questioned, but somehow they were conveniently ig-nored or circumvented. There was a good reason for this attitude: the colonies were run from Spain, and it often took years for messages to be sent and decisions to be made and communicated. Meanwhile, everyday government had to go on in the colonies, and go on it did, without too much concern for the letter of the law.

Thus the Spanish attitude toward the law was intensified by Latin American circumstances. However, it is still alive and well in Spain today. Spain is still inordinately bureau-cratic, and ordinary citizens respond by trying to get around the system. They seek out loopholes whenever possible, as reflected in a Spanish proverb: Hecha la ley, hecha la trampa, which means "Every law has its loophole." This is the way things appear to work in Spain, much to the discomfort of Americans. Computerization has brought change, but slowly. For instance, Spaniards continue to be quite contemptuous of parking tickets. City dwellers collect sheaves of unpaid tick-ets, which they have no intention of doing anything about. Why should they? It's the city's fault if the citizens park illegally—there should be more parking places or parking garages.

Parking tickets bring out all the pícaro in many Spaniards. The pícaro is a Spanish folk figure who first appeared in literary form in the anonymous sixteenth-century work, La vida de Lazarillo de Tormes y de sus fortunas y adversidades (The Life of Lazarillo de Tormes and His Adventures and Adversities). Lazarillo de Tormes was a young boy who served a number of masters, including a blind man, an impoverished knight, and a priest. The book is the tale of his adventures and misfortunes. The creed by which the boy lived was "Look out for yourself"—and he did, through thick and thin. Lazarillo was only the first of many pícaros to appear in Spanish literature, and the word pícaro, which can only unsatisfactorily be translated as "rascal," lives on in contemporary Spanish.

The pícaro also surfaces when Spaniards have to deal with taxes. For tax purposes, they routinely declare the value of real estate they have bought at slightly more than half the real value. Everyone knows this: the person selling, the person buying, the real estate agents, the notary, and presumably Hacienda (the Spanish Treasury). The thought of such blatant disregard for the law puts many Americans in a cold sweat. Even though forms of petty tax fraud are also practiced by Americans, they aren't so flagrant about it. Entry into the European Union brought a new type of tax: the IVA, or Value-Added Tax. With it came another tax collection problem—people were failing to pay up. Spaniards avoid paying IVA, just as they understate property values and refuse to pay parking tickets, because they feel they are not getting their money's worth in government services. In their eyes, government is quick to take but slow to give back as it should. Many Americans feel the same way: witness the perennial popularity of tax-cap initiatives in local and state elections. However, where an American pays the tax but supports the anti-tax initiative, a Spaniard doesn't pay the tax.

The issue of smoking on Spanish trains also points up the complex relationship between the individual and the law in Spain. Smoking was forbidden on trains when Franco was alive, but after his death people started smoking wherever they pleased. Then Renfe (the Spanish railway company) prohibited smoking again in all carriages and put up "No Smoking" signs—but ashtrays were left in place, and people continued smoking. Later, Renfe again changed the rules and provided both smoking and nonsmoking carriages. People went on smoking wherever and whenever they wished. If someone pointed out that smoking was prohibited, they invariably said, *"Es igual"* ("It's all the same") and asserted that they didn't care what the sign said. But if asked to stop smoking because it bothered other people, they would stop. Nowadays there is more respect for posted signs (although smoking is so widespread that secondhand smoke is extremely pervasive). Nonetheless, Spaniards tend to assume that rules and regulations are somewhat flexible. This contrasts sharply with the American willingness to obey impersonal laws and regulations. Spaniards have an aversion to obeying bureaucratic rules and regulations; a personal request is more real and more important.

Another example of differing perceptions of regulations occurred in a multinational company in Barcelona. The company cafeteria, in accordance with American regulations, was dry; no alcohol was allowed. One day a major corporate deadline had been met early, and it was announced that work would end early and there would be a celebration in the cafeteria. The Spanish staff automatically went out and bought bottles of *cava* (Catalan champagne), without which no party is complete. For the Spaniards, the no-alcohol rule was one thing, but cava at a party was another. However, when the American managers arrived, they saw only a breach of company rules and ordered the offending bottles removed.

Still another example of the difference between Spanish and American attitudes in regard to rules and regulations is exam-taking behavior. Americans who teach Spaniards learn that at exam time Spaniards will invariably look at one another's papers unless the seating arrangements in the room actively prevent it. Everyone does this—the best-prepared students as well as the worst-prepared. Even the terminology of this behavior is significantly different: Spaniards call it *copiar* (copying), a far more neutral term than the American word *cheating*, which carries a strong connotation of moral disapproval. Many an American teacher has been reduced to helpless fury by the sight of students sitting side by side, blatantly looking at one another's exam papers. Americans see this behavior as dishonorable; Spaniards merely see it as practical: "Everyone copies in exams, and if you don't want us to, you should separate the chairs."

Spanish students are used to a system in which, among other things, they may be examined on material not taught during the course. Exams are often arbitrary, unfair, skewed, or designed to make a certain number of students fail. Given this, copying becomes a logical form of self-protection. Two Americans in an M.B.A. program in Barcelona said that one of the things they learned was to copy in exams. The workload was excessive; the content of exams was unpredictable and arbitrary; and when the choice was to fail (unfairly) or to copy, they copied. They didn't cheat, which implies dishonest use of a fair system. Rather, they copied, which implies necessary self-protection from an unfair system.

To understand this behavior one must return again to the colonial mindset of obedezco, pero no cumplo. What the colonial period had in common with the present, or at least the recent past, was the arbitrariness of laws and regulations, in the face of which the individual was impotent. Authority was often equivalent to repression, and the only way left open to the individual was that of the pícaro. One of the hardest tasks for the government of Spain during the years since the restoration of democracy has been to rebuild the individual's confidence that government is made up of human beings who are accountable, of laws that can be modified or thrown out, and of institutions that are there to serve the people and not vice versa.

A change in Spanish mentality regarding government and the law will not occur overnight. Spaniards still have to be convinced of what Americans believe implicitly, that the system can be fought. When Americans in Spain stand up for their rights, their Spanish friends often try to dissuade them, saying, "You're just a private individual. You can't change the system." If Americans do effect change, Spaniards react with amazement and perhaps with a sneaking suspicion that being American helped.

These attitudes toward law and authority constitute a profound difference between Spaniards and Americans. The Americans who have come to terms with this difference are those who understand the mentality and its origins and recognize that the "American way" cannot automatically be transplanted to another society with a different history and different traditions. The rise of armed extremism in the United States has also reminded Americans that some of their compatriots feel exempt from the laws of the nation.

Confianza: *Trust in Spanish Society*

The arrival of warm spring weather in Spanish cities brings with it several characteristic sights: the swallows that nest in the eaves of buildings and swoop through the air at early morning and dusk; the outdoor café tables where people sit and eat or drink at all hours; the tour buses with flocks of tourists being shepherded to the sights; and then some of these same tourists, reporting to their respective consulates or embassies that their wallets have been stolen or their purses snatched. To the angry tourist who has lost passport, money, tickets, and traveler's checks and has had a vacation ruined, Spain is a dangerous place. Levels of both unemployment and drug addiction are high in Spanish cities, contributing to petty crime, especially street crime. The tourist, of course, is easy prey anywhere. Residents blend in, both in appearance and in behavior, and know where not to go and how to spot trouble coming, though they too can be the victims of theft or other crime in Spain.

What is striking, however, is that most Americans living in Spain tend to comment not so much on the incidence of crime as on the extent to which Spanish society seems to run on *confianza. Confianza* means not confidence but trust. *Una persona de confianza* is a person who can be trusted. Perhaps the longevity and stability of work relationships and the fact that so many Spaniards are living and working in the town where they and their families have always lived contributes to the importance of confianza. In a stable environment, reputation is very important. It is possible that Americans who move to Spain are already so far away from their hometowns that they have lost touch with this kind of relationship, which is by no means unique to Spain.

In the United States, as elsewhere, the corner store where you buy a paper every day is more likely to let you owe a dollar than the department store where you are just one of thousands of customers per week. Spain is no different in this regard. However, what surprises Americans is how quickly they can obtain people's trust, even when a considerable amount of money is involved. In one instance, an American resident in Barcelona had to make three plane reservations from Barcelona to Germany for family members. The cost was substantial and the American could get only a part of it out of the bank in one day with his cash card, yet the tickets had to be issued and paid for that day. His solution was to ask some fellow Americans at his office to lend him the money until the next day, when he could withdraw more from the bank. Overhearing him, one of his Spanish colleagues said, "Do they know you at the travel agency?"

"Well, I've been there before."

"Then there shouldn't be any problem. Ask the travel agency if you can give them what you have as a deposit and then pay the difference tomorrow. They're bound to say yes if they know you."

Sure enough, the travel agency issued the plane tickets without full payment.

Spain abounds with this type of anecdote. Hotel clerks accept room reservations over the telephone without asking for a credit card number as a guarantee. Checks may be accepted without identification, even though the writer's name, address, and phone number are not routinely printed on Spanish checks. Many neighborhood grocery stores keep a notebook with the names of people who maintain accounts at the store and often shop without money. *Ya me lo pagará mañana* (You can pay me tomorrow) is a common phrase.

Americans often find Spanish confianza very pleasant, but it can also make them uncomfortable because they are not accustomed to this style of dealing with people. An American trained in a U.S. corporate culture may balk, for instance, at Spanish interviewing and hiring procedures, which tend to rely much more on whether the person and his or her family are known and are de confianza than on the details of education and professional background, the appearance of the résumé, and the number and quality of letters of recommendation. Similarly, an American entering into contract negotiations may be disconcerted at the amount of information that is taken for granted or left unclear. Spaniards often feel there is no need to pore over details, since everything can be worked out satisfactorily as long as the person one is dealing with is de confianza.

To Americans, this reliance on confianza is often perceived as being inefficient. The person who is de confianza may be wrong for the job. Negotiations frequently leave the way open for later confusion, misunderstandings, and mistakes because verbal agreements based on confianza, rather than hard bargaining carefully translated into written contracts, have been forgotten or misremembered.

Americans living in Spain must walk a fine line here. On the one hand, Spaniards admire American efficiency and detail consciousness. On the other hand, the American who persists in imposing the American style, who demands too many letters of recommendation or insists on every detail in writing, may appear overly suspicious and lacking in trust. The other side of giving trust is that one also expects to receive it; Spaniards who know themselves to be de confianza will be offended by suspicion.

Americans often do not really trust Spaniards to attend to detail and to remember everything that has been said or to judge accurately a person's abilities or qualifications when there is not much written evidence to back them up. However, if the American is not careful, the Spaniards will perceive this mistrust in a much more global sense, as an imputation that they are basically untrustworthy people, which in most cases is not the intention of the American. But serious trouble can result when Spaniards feel their character has been impugned. The best thing Americans can do in these situations is to slacken their pace, pin down as much detail as possible without communicating mistrust, and then back off. What is not worked out to the last detail in one meeting can be worked out in the next or the following. It is usually better to postpone something than to alienate people critical to your operation. It is also helpful in these situations if Americans don't take themselves too seriously. In asking for more details, they might say something like, "You know how Americans are; we like every detail to be down on paper," thereby distancing themselves emotionally from their professional attitudes. What they are really saying, though not in so many words, is, "This is the way people in my culture do things, and even if you think it's foolish, I can't help being a foolish American, so why don't you humor me?" This will make it easier for the Spaniards, in turn, to distance themselves from their own emotional reactions and to say to one another, "Well, they're just being American; let's humor them," as opposed to "What's wrong with them? Why are they being so American?"

---

[1] Diaz-Plaja, *Seven Deadly Sins*, 56–57.

Encounter Two: Por Regla General

Kathy runs the library attached to a U.S. consulate in Spain. One day a student asks about art schools in the United States. Kathy recommends a directory listing different schools and colleges, and the student spends several hours looking through it and copying down information. When Kathy starts closing the library for the day, the student asks if she can check out the directory, since she won't be able to visit the library again until next week. Kathy says that according to library policy, reference books cannot be checked out. The student won't take no for an answer. She persists and, in the face of Kathy's repeated refusals, grows indignant and finally demands to see Kathy's supervisor. Kathy loses her patience and says, "It's the rule and that's all," and holds the door open. The student leaves, muttering angrily about Americans. How could Kathy have resolved such an encounter more gracefully?

Spanish people are casual about regulations. When dealing with a person, they expect there to be some room for negotiation and react angrily if the person just keeps repeating the regulation.

Kathy would have obtained better results first, by explaining why the regulation exists—directories are expensive to replace if lost, and the information needs to be readily available to library patrons at all times. Second, she could have discussed the problem from the student's viewpoint—she could come back next week, or send a friend or relative tomorrow.

The process of explanation and discussion would make Kathy's refusal much more acceptable. Spaniards say "Hablando, la gente se entiende" (Discussion is the way to understanding). By participating in a discussion, Kathy should be able to forestall both the student's indignation and her own resentment. If all else fails, she should be ready with her supervisor's name. "¿Con quién tengo que hablar?" ("Who do I need to talk to?") is a common question from Spaniards who don't get their own way.

3

Relationships

Dramatic contrasts exist between Spanish and American styles of pursuing and maintaining close relationships. Friendship patterns, sex roles, and relationships between men and women vary markedly between the two cultures and are frequent causes of misunderstanding and conflict when Spaniards and Americans encounter each other. These issues are discussed in detail in this chapter.

Friendship Patterns

Making Friends

The mobility and change typical of life in the United States play a major role in determining the nature of American friendship patterns. Because Americans move from place to place and change jobs frequently, they develop the ability to establish new relationships quickly and easily. This is accomplished in a variety of ways: in school; through one's job, hobbies, or club life; at parties; through church or temple; and by participating in sports. One of the reasons this process is quick and easy is that Americans often compartmentalize their relationships into friends from work, friends from the team, and so on.

One American social habit that facilitates an immediate rapport with a new acquaintance is that of asking personal questions and volunteering personal information. So ingrained is this in the American style that the formation of phrases and questions about personal matters is a part of every basic course in American English for foreigners. Spaniards, like many Europeans, are made uncomfortable by this barrage of personal questions and information.

For Spaniards, making friends follows a very different pattern. Children usually spend all their school years in the same school with the same friends, and if they go to college, it is usually in their home city, and very often with at least some of their friends from school. Starting a new job is a time to make new friends for Spaniards as for Americans, but most Spaniards do not change jobs very often. For most Spanish men, the period of compulsory military service is the only time when they will associate with a wholly new group of people. As for church, it is often far less of a social institution than in the United States, and the percentage of regular churchgoers is lower in Spain than in the U.S. Finally, parties are not the same. In Spain groups of people who already know one another go out together. If the organizer of the evening has invited people who do not know one another, the chances are that at the end of the evening they still will not know one another. Only at a second or third meeting will they begin to learn names and chat, but they are unlikely to establish a relationship independently of the person who originally brought them together. When Americans living in Spain throw parties, inviting everyone they know and expecting them to mingle, the Spanish guests typically arrive in groups which stay together for the whole evening, often causing the American hosts considerable bewilderment or frustration.

When Spaniards go on vacation, they become expansive and friendly, easily striking up conversations and acquaintanceships with strangers. Americans can relate to this with no difficulty. However, when fall comes, the summer lifestyle disappears. Spending a summer vacation at a beach resort in Spain is no preparation for living year-round in a big Spanish city. This is a trap into which many foreigners have fallen, and many a midwinter depression has been the result.

Friendship and Intimacy

In Spain, as in the United States, people have a circle of casual friends and a few soulmates. American and Spanish friendship patterns differ most where casual friendships are concerned.

Because Spaniards typically experience little change in their lives, even casual friends remain in the picture for years. However, the fact that a friendship is of long standing does not necessarily make it intimate, as illustrated by the *tertulia*. Traditionally this was a circle of male friends who met regularly in a bar or restaurant (since Spanish homes are much less open to outsiders than American homes). The purpose of the tertulia was to sit and talk—about literature, current events, bullfighting, soccer, or whatever. The most famous tertulias included people prominent in letters or public life. The traditional tertulia was a male institution, perhaps because men had the leisure to sit around in cafés talking and women were not encouraged to do so. Today's tertulia occurs mostly in the setting of radio and television talk shows, which carry on the tradition in more than name, bringing together a variety of experts and characters whose opinions delight their loyal following.

What was very Spanish about the traditional tertulia was that people could belong to one for years, seeing one another almost daily, and yet know very little about one another's personal lives. This characterizes many casual friendships in Spain. With casual friends, Spaniards talk about current events and other people but not about private matters, deeply held beliefs, or problems. What these relationships may lack in depth they make up for in longevity. Spaniards feel they know someone well because they have known them a long time, not because they know everything about them.

The Spanish lifestyle is conducive to maintaining a dense network of long-term relationships. In general, changes occur less frequently, work pressures are less intense, schedules are more relaxed, and family commitments are less restrictive. For example, a Spanish woman might receive a phone call at work from a former coworker she hasn't seen in years but who was able to locate her easily because she has not changed jobs. They agree to meet for a drink after work the following day, because she has nothing else on her calendar. She arranges for a friend or family member to pick up her child from day care and meets her former coworker at the appointed place. After an hour's conversation they part, agreeing to meet again more often, and she goes home to tell her husband about her pleasant social encounter. This scenario would be less likely for two American women.

Americans find it easy to establish casual friendships with Spaniards but hard to get any farther. It can be frustrating for Americans to find that after a few months in Spain, all they seem to have are acquaintances to share coffee or drinks with. They may find conversations superficial and gossipy and feel friendships are going nowhere.

Americans in Spain lack the family support most Spaniards take for granted, and they therefore expect more intimacy in their friendships. Americans also tend to rush friendships, expecting instant results rather than letting friendships slowly ripen.

Many Americans in Spain find their first friends among other Americans, who provide help and moral support through the initial period of language difficulties and culture shock. They provide "instant friendship" while relationships with Spaniards are getting established. As these develop, more of a balance is usually achieved between Spanish and American friends.

Americans leaving Spain often find it much harder to say good-bye to Spanish friends than to American friends. Other Americans can easily accept that friendships change with circumstances. They may exchange holiday cards or occasional phone calls or e-mail, but often the relationship is over as soon as constant contact ceases. Spaniards find this fickle. In Spain, friends are for keeps. It is not unusual for men who became friends in the *mili* (military service) to maintain that friendship through life. Spaniards are typically disconsolate at the prospect of saying good-bye to a friend.

Relationships in the Workplace

Job mobility is low in Spain, especially at middle and lower organizational levels. One reason for this is the consistently high level of unemployment; when jobs are hard to find, people tend to stay with the one they have. Another factor is the difficulty an organization has in getting rid of a contracted employee. Labor laws protect employees from dismissal, and firing someone involves either accumulating a complicated series of written admonitions based on documented offenses or else paying off the dismissed employee with one or two years' salary. People who do not like their jobs or who do them badly may nonetheless hang on for years, both because they cannot be dismissed and because they prefer the security of the present job to the risk involved in trying to find another.

Partly as a result of this low job mobility, an atmosphere of intimacy and unity among Spanish coworkers usually prevails. People spend many hours not only working side by side but also eating together and socializing during the long lunch breaks (at least two hours) that Spain, in the old Mediterranean tradition, continues to have. While in the past this enabled people to go home, eat, and perhaps have a siesta during the lunch break, city dwellers today live too far away from work to go home. Many coworkers have lunch together every day, taking advantage of the *menú del día* (daily special) at nearby restaurants, which often have certain tables permanently reserved for the lunchtime regulars. Adding up working hours and the long lunch hours, many Spaniards spend up to ten hours a day in one another's company. It is therefore not surprising that coworkers become not only friends, in the American sense, but family, in the Spanish sense; that is, they know a great deal about one another's personal lives and have shared many personal and professional ups and downs. Ironically, even rivals and enemies are a stable part of the work environment, a fact that can create challenges for managers (see chapter 5).

This atmosphere of intimacy and trust in the workplace is important to Spaniards, and it directly affects their reactions to the expectations and practices Americans bring there. For instance, Americans are usually task oriented. They feel that they have come to do a job and tend to concentrate on it rather than on cultivating relationships with coworkers. What they fail to realize is that these relationships will powerfully influence their ability to get the job done. Americans who neglect to establish good relationships at work may find a lack of cooperation that eventually undermines their effectiveness. This is a dilemma because the American task orientation and "Let's get this show on the road" attitude is also something Spaniards admire. However, it is one thing to admire an attribute that leads to greater efficiency and productivity and another to work every day with a person who is insensitive to good relations in the office. Spaniards may like what Americans accomplish without liking how they act, especially if they are poor at integrating into the *familia*.

Why do Americans act as they do? It may be partly because, even though they normally make friends easily, they feel their time in Spain is going to be so short that it is not worth the effort to develop good relations. Selection for foreign assignments is still based overwhelmingly on technical ability and rank rather than social skills. Also, Americans are often brought in to show, to teach, to manage, and/or to lead. The implied message, especially in the thinking of the American head office, is that no Spaniard could do the job as well. Conscious of this, Americans may feel that they are under hostile observation. It is often said that *envidia* (jealousy, envy) is the Spanish vice and that Spaniards prefer to backbite and criticize rather than to openly compete. But in a work environment where people cannot be fired, open confrontation with coworkers may lead to feuding rather than clearing the air; therefore, people keep resentments to themselves. Also, how can Spaniards openly compete with imported Americans who are also superiors in the hierarchy? Rather, they will observe the Americans, take their measure, and then treat them accordingly—with trust or suspicion, openness or reserve—depending on the atmosphere the American has created. One Spanish employee of an American multinational corporation said, "*Aqui hay blancos, negritos, y negritos con cualificaciones.*" (In this company there are white folks, darkies, and darkies with qualifications.) It may seem that way to many Spaniards, and whether it proves to be true or not will be influenced by the attitude of the current *blanco*.

Americans, meanwhile, may be wary of integrating, and if this wariness is interpreted as standoffishness, the imagined hostility may become real. First, the feeling of having to "show their stuff" may bring out the competitiveness in Americans. They may see the Spanish staff as rivals, even if they are subordinates, and there will probably be an element of truth in this. Those Spaniards who are qualified and motivated probably do look forward to the day when they can be in the Americans' shoes. However, in the Spanish work environment competitiveness is seen as negative whenever it interferes with good working relationships. People are not expected to compete openly for preference or advancement. Therefore, Americans who are trying to dazzle their Spanish colleagues may only be impressing them with how unpleasant they are.

Second, the Americans' loyalties and networks are often with the parent company, rather than with the local branch or office. Most Americans will eventually go home, and they cannot afford to let their contacts cool or to get out of touch with events and trends back home. Nonetheless, if they want to succeed in Spain, Americans must be committed and loyal to the local office. Only in this way will they get commitment and loyalty in return.

Sex Roles

Latin Lovers

On arriving in Spain, the American may soon observe—or experience—the *piropo*. The dictionary discreetly defines *piropo* as "a compliment" or "flattery," but that definition falls far short of describing what happens. A piropo is a suggestive remark called out by a man to any passing woman. American men find this reminiscent of low-class behavior at home. American women find it galling. The piropo, also found in other southern European cultures, is usually the American woman's first experience of the "Latin Lover" syndrome in Spain.

The Latin Lover is now something of a joke in Spain. Pronounced with a caricature of a Spanish accent—*Lateen Loberr*—it recalls the era when Spain first became the summer playground of Europe. At that time northern European and American women who came to Spanish beach resorts in the summer represented societies where women were far more liberated than in Spain. A myth sprang up around *suecas* (Swedish women) which became the umbrella term for all blonde foreign women. Because of the free-and-easy holiday mood and the greater degree of sexual freedom of their cultures, suecas were equated with loose morals. Men who worked in hotels, restaurants, and discotheques at the beach resorts were reputed to have their pick of sex-mad foreign females. Even today, with Spanish women as liberated as their northern neighbors and bare-breasted women all over Spanish beaches, television still feeds the sueca fantasy of blonde foreign beach goddesses. This myth does nothing to make life easier for foreign women who visit Spain to study, see the sights, or make friends.

Don Juan, perhaps the original Latin Lover, first appeared in literature in *El burlador de Sevilla* (The Deceiver from Seville) by Tirso de Molina (1571–1648). Don Juan (based on a real person) and his seductive prowess caught the imagination of Europe and has since appeared in countless forms. Spain does not have a monopoly on the Latin Lover. However, males in Spanish society have traditionally been prized from birth; pampered during childhood and adolescence; and, in adult life, privileged with more personal freedom, social authority, and economic power than women. *Machismo* is the cult of the male and male sexist behavior. However, Don Juan is as much the object of satire as he is of admiration in today's Spain.

Don Juan may be only an old story and the Latin Lover an overplayed myth, but there is no doubt that the differences between Spanish and American sex roles and relationships can create problems in male-female interactions.

Americans tend to enter romantic relationships and marriage on their own, without depending on their families for support and sometimes even without family involvement. If problems arise, the couple may seek help from professional counselors; if the problems persist, the marriage is dissolved. Spaniards, like many foreigners, are struck by the speed with which some American couples move from the wedding reception to the divorce court. This pattern of relationships reflects certain values and attitudes shared by most Americans: the assumption that an individual is responsible for his or her own life, the idealistic belief that somehow one can (or should) make one's own life situation perfect, and a certain intolerance for ambiguous or contradictory circumstances.

In Spain, male-female relationships have traditionally been

influenced by the definition—common in Latin countries—
of woman's role as either mother or mistress. Until a generation ago, Spanish women were expected to be very conscious
of personal appearance only until marriage. Once they were
married and particularly once children arrived, women were
expected to embrace the mother role completely. It was faintly
improper for a married Spanish woman to watch her weight
or to dress in youthful fashions. Meanwhile, many husbands
found other women to play the mistress role. Wives often
knew of these liaisons but could do nothing about them,
principally because divorce was unobtainable. Support from
the extended family and her social status as a married woman
helped many a Spanish woman to live with a situation that
would have driven her American counterpart to the divorce
court. For Spaniards under forty, the situation has changed
considerably. The legalization of divorce has given both men
and women an escape from unacceptable marriages. However, an American would still be quicker than a Spaniard to
label a situation "unacceptable."

In particular, Spaniards are more accepting than Americans of extramarital relationships. Both spouses may maintain friendships with people they knew and dated before
marriage. Some men still have mistresses whom they support
financially and visit regularly. Spaniards are mystified that in
the United States the discovery of extramarital adventures
can derail a career. In Spain, if scandal attaches to a public
figure, it concerns financial or political matters, never sexual
partners. Revealing that a prominent politician had a mistress would be an example of "Dog Bites Man."

An American male teacher married to a Spanish woman
was surprised to find that his female students, knowing he
was married, nonetheless flirted with him. For the American,
flirting with a married man was the first step to what could be
serious involvement and the termination of his marriage. For
the students, flirting was an amusement that probably would
not lead to serious involvement and even if it did would not
affect the marriage.

Single American women complain of the lack of a singles scene in Spain, which is explained in part by the fact that many couples still stay together for the sake of extended family or children. In other words, the number of older singles is much smaller in Spain than in the United States, although the divorce rate is on the rise. Many American women find they are expected to play the role of mistress, or else go out with far younger men who are not yet married. It is a hard choice: loneliness or a relationship Americans find unequal or dishonest.

As for American single men in Spain, some have also found the mistress-mother divide still firmly in place. One man entered what he believed to be an easy, freewheeling affair with a Spanish woman and was shocked when she announced she was pregnant and expected him to marry her. American men looking to get married have traditionally had no problem in Spain. Those looking for no-strings-attached relationships do better nowadays with divorced women, who are most likely to have outgrown the mistress-mother mindset.

Change and Conflict

The changes that have taken place in Spain over the last fifteen to twenty years are nowhere more evident than in relationships between the sexes. Anyone who visited Spain as recently as the early 1970s still found that female tourists were not allowed into churches if they were clad in shorts and were required to wear shawls to cover bare shoulders. In the same period, it was still *un escándalo público* (a public scandal) for a couple to kiss in public, and they could be arrested for doing so. As John Hooper remarks in *The New Spaniards*,[1] when one sees young women walking around on Spanish beaches nowadays, wearing only the skimpiest of bikini bottoms and nothing else, it is hard to imagine that their mothers were probably chaperoned whenever they went out in public.

These changes have come about partly because of changes in the law. In the years following the Constitution of 1978, divorce and abortion were legalized. Furthermore, contraception became more accessible, resulting in a dramatic drop in the average number of children per woman of childbearing age, now one of the lowest in the industrialized world.

With such rapid and far-reaching changes, conflict has been inevitable. For example, two middle-aged Spanish women of the same age and background could display radically different feelings about their children's relationships. One mother was humiliated by her son's civil marriage to a divorced woman. In her eyes a nonreligious ceremony had no validity, and she was determined not to rest until her new daughter-in-law obtained an annulment of her first marriage, thus legitimizing the second marriage in the eyes of the church. In contrast, the other mother did not turn a hair when her daughter took off for weekend camping trips with her boyfriend. "I'm sure they know what they're doing" was her only comment.

One thing that surprises foreigners who still believe Spanish society has a strict Catholic moral code is the large, vocal, and sophisticated gay community in Spain, especially male homosexuals. Sitges, on the Catalan coast, is an international gay resort, and in the summer the beach is carefully demarcated into the "family" section and the "boys'" section. Similarly, Carnival in Sitges and nearby Villanova is celebrated during the day by costumed bands of children and at night by men in the wildest of drag outfits. Homosexuality is a common part of Spanish life, and this casts a different light on the outsider's concept of a society dominated by traditional males.

Contrasts such as the one between the family beach and the boys' beach in Sitges abound in modern Spain. Despite a recent swing back to the fashion of white church weddings, there are still a number of public figures in Spain who are single parents or divorcés or are living with people to whom they are not married. Though commonplace in today's world, such lifestyles are surprising in a society that also has regular vigils and processions in honor of the Virgin Mary advertised with slogans such as *Catholics: come and honor your Holy Mother.*

Still another source of conflict, or at least tension, is the increasing number of women working outside the home. Great pressures have been brought to bear when work schedule and responsibilities conflict with, or are added to, the work and responsibilities of running a home and raising children.

Changes in laws and social customs have opened up greater educational and professional opportunities for Spanish women over the past generation. Beginning with the 1978 Constitution and its guarantees of equal rights and equal opportunity for women, a steady stream of legislation has addressed the traditional gender inequities of Spanish society. The legalization of divorce and abortion were followed by official Plans of Equal Opportunities for women. The enrollment of women in higher education has increased 40 percent since 1991. Predictably, more education leads to higher expectations in both the professional and personal arenas. As in the United States, such expectations may clash with existing realities, and young people are most likely to demand equal treatment without compromise.

Feminists still find much to criticize in the situation of Spanish women. Women are much less likely than a generation ago to be harassed on the street by men calling out piropos. However, sexual harassment in the workplace and spousal abuse at home are both widespread. Although they have become an issue for public debate and legislation, women who endure these attacks still cannot call upon as much social support, legal muscle, and practical assistance as women in the United States.

Men and Women at Home

In the past, as in most traditional cultures, the woman took care of the home, the children, and the meals, while the man went out to work. In today's world, however, a great number of Spanish women work outside the home. As a result, men's and women's roles are in transition, as they are in other countries. In some families, men continue to regard home and child rearing as the exclusive preserve of the woman. This produces the *doble jornada* (double shift) for women who combine full-time employment with their other jobs as mother and homemaker. Other couples reach a more equitable arrangement, with both man and woman sharing joint responsibilities to a much greater extent. Sometimes within a single family married siblings may have different household arrangements, with one brother being a typical *machista* (male chauvinist) and refusing to lift a finger in the home, while another does some of the cooking and shopping or his share of taking care of the baby. In this respect male and female roles in Spain vary as much as in the United States, making any generalizations impossible.

Spaniards are proud of their homes and want them to be nicely decorated and well kept. Americans, seeing the often dingy exteriors of Spanish apartment buildings, are usually surprised to see how house- proud Spaniards are and how picture-perfect their apartments can be.

Spanish perceptions of the American home are influenced by what they see on television shows. Many Spaniards think that a proper home, with regular meals and family life, can no longer be found in the United States. Spaniards often think of the American woman as being completely cut off from the traditional role of the homemaker—as someone who neither cooks nor cleans, who depends on fast food, frozen dinners, and maid service. These Spaniards would be amazed to find out how many American women still bake cookies and drive the kids to Little League. Such women are not the stuff of internationally marketed television shows. Women who come to Spain on professional assignments have usually left the cookies-and-kiddies option far behind, and they can be critical and unsympathetic about what they see as the enslavement of Spanish women who are juggling home, family, and work. If, in addition, these American women cannot cook or do not "run a nice home," they serve as confirmation of the Spanish theory of the deterioration of home life in the United States.

Both the U.S. and Spanish societies are dealing with the same problem: conflict between the traditional structure in the home and the new realities of two-career couples. It will be easier for Americans to accept that the situation in Spain is not so different from that in the United States if they can manage to see the underlying similarities beneath the surface differences of machista style.

Men and Women at Work

There are inconsistencies in the Spanish workplace just as there are in the Spanish home. On the one hand, Spanish women are mayors, presidents of companies, and high-ranking government officials. On the other hand, they are still grappling with workplace issues such as unequal pay, unequal advancement opportunities, and sexual harassment. These problems are contrary to the constitutional rights of women in Spain, but, as is the case in the United States, there is a gap between the law and its application, and the process for taking a case to court is long, complicated, and expensive.

Americans are surprised to see job descriptions and employment advertisements in Spain that specify the gender of applicants without fear of legal repercussions, although gender-neutral language is becoming more common. Clear demarcation of gender roles at work has traditionally helped to rationalize pay inequities between men and women. Today, young women are seeking the same training and opportunities as men, demanding to step outside traditional work roles, and knocking on the glass ceiling.

Examples abound of male-female distinctions that many Americans would see as sexist. A contact person in an organization is identified as, for example, Señor González (if a man) but as Señorita Rosa (if a woman)—that is, using the man's surname but the woman's first name. Most Spanish men addressing a woman for the first time will ask, "*¿Señora o señorita?*"

Americans working in Spanish offices may be surprised at the familiarity between workers of opposite sexes. New clothes and haircuts are the subject of detailed comment and analysis. Women are constantly receiving piropos, which are sometimes reciprocated. Often such treatment is part of the familia atmosphere, built on the trust of long acquaintanceship. At the same time, sexual harassment has long been a feature of the Spanish workplace, with attractive young women considered fair game. In the United States, changes in behavior have been driven by changes in the law, followed by lawsuits. In Spain, sexual harassment now has a name (*acoso sexual*) and is the topic of public debate and legislation.

---

[1] John Hooper, *The New Spaniards* (New York: Penguin USA, 1995), 189.

Encounter Three: Desconocido

Ben moves into his new apartment in a Spanish city. He soon locates a tobacco shop and goes in to buy stamps, carrying a stack of postcards and letters to mail to people back home. He is waited on by an attractive, well-dressed young woman. Impressed by her appearance, Ben tries out his best Spanish and all his charm, but her manner remains cool and distant. Though she has to spend some time weighing the letters and looking up the postal rates, she does not ask him where he is from or what he is doing in Spain. However, while waiting on him she greets other customers with a smile. How should Ben interpret the shop assistant's behavior?

A. She doesn't like Americans.

B. She is offended by his imperfect Spanish.

C. She is a rude and unfriendly person.

D. She doesn't know him.

A. *It is possible, but there is no reason to assume this.*

B. *This option is unlikely, since Spaniards are not touchy about foreigners speaking their language.*

C. *Only if the shop assistant is judged by American expectations could this be a reasonable option.*

D. *This interpretation is the most likely, especially as the assistant is only chilly with Ben and is friendly with other customers.*

COMMENT: The shop assistant, a young and attractive single woman, would not be "friendly" in the American sense to any stranger, particularly a male. Asking personal questions is generally avoided in Spain, and more so as she is not trying to strike up an acquaintance. She feels much more obligated to her regular customers, who are already being made to wait because she has to take so much time with Ben. He is likely to receive more amiable treatment once he, too, becomes a regular customer.

-

4

Language and Communication

Learning Spanish

Americans going to Spain should definitely know something of Castilian. Any American who doubts this need only think about the plight of a foreigner who arrives in the United States unable to speak English. Even though some of their Spanish colleagues will speak English, both Spaniards and Americans in Spain agree that Americans who are unable to communicate in Castilian are at a great disadvantage. Some of the kinds of cross-cultural misunderstandings noted in this book can be exacerbated to the point of conflict if there is also a serious language barrier. Furthermore, it is generally agreed that a one-month crash course in beginner's or tourist Castilian, though better than nothing, is insufficient. Americans who can reach an intermediate level of language proficiency, however, will be able to cope satisfactorily from their first day in Spain and learn from what is going on around them. One of the most popular myths about language learning is that the best way to learn a language is to "just go to the country and immerse yourself in it." People who have tried this approach without prior knowledge of the language agree that they condemned themselves to feeling totally incompetent for a full year. Most Americans arriving in Spain for professional reasons do not have the luxury of sounding like a fool, even for a week. Since instruction in Castilian is easily accessible in the United States, it is difficult to understand why corporations still send their high-ranking officials to Spain without equipping them with the language.

Obviously, corporate goals cannot always wait on language classes, and the individual with the necessary know-how for an assignment in Spain may not be the one with the best knowledge of Castilian. Nonetheless, it would probably be better in the long run for the achievement of the company's purposes and for the well-being of the person being sent to Spain if departure were postponed to allow for three months of intensive language training, as is common practice among Spanish executives, students, or other visitors going to the United States.

It is important as well for Americans to continue studying Castilian once in Spain, since regular classes will help them make sense of the language that is bombarding them from all sides. It can also be a good public relations move, as will be discussed later.

One comfort for Americans studying Castilian is that Spaniards are typically tolerant of foreigners trying to learn their language, in contrast, for example, to the French, whose ideal of linguistic perfection leads them to be quite demanding and critical of foreigners who speak French poorly. Spaniards may tease Americans about their accents, but the ribbing is good-natured. For the most part they are patient and will often gently correct and explain mistakes to help the learning process along.

With respect to the other languages of Spain, the position of Castilian-speaking Americans is quite delicate and depends on the length of their stay. As we have noted, the language issue in Spain is highly political and tied closely with the issue of regional autonomy. Many Basques and Catalans in particular think of themselves as belonging to nations that have been conquered or occupied by Spain.

Their language is an outward sign of nationhood. Such strong feelings may be quite difficult for Americans to understand, but they are real and should not be taken lightly.

Speakers of regional languages normally assume that if a newly arrived foreigner speaks anything, it will be Castilian. Nonetheless, bilingual Spaniards very often slip into their own languages, even when there is someone present who is theoretically not expected to understand. Americans may feel offended by this, thinking that they are deliberately being excluded or that this implies criticism about their lack of knowledge of the language. Spaniards who speak only Castilian also feel excluded and resentful when Euskera or Catalan are spoken in their presence.

Speakers of regional languages protest that it is not their intention to exclude others, and that use of these languages is not only a right but also central to their identity. Outlawed during the Franco era, the regional languages were used only in private settings. Now that a whole new generation has been educated bilingually, use of Euskera, Catalan, and Gallego is ever more widespread in business, the arts, and the media. Americans who settle into one of the bilingual areas of Spain for more than a year or two may find that the pressure to speak the regional language is greater. By staying longer, the foreigner is making a visible commitment to the place, and the natives tend to feel that learning the regional language is part of that commitment. An American musician who joined an orchestra in Barcelona found that everyone spoke to him in Catalan, though they said magnanimously that he could speak to them in Castilian if he liked!

In Catalonia there is another reason for this pressure. The massive immigration of the 1960s brought people from other parts of Spain to Catalonia. Poverty-stricken villagers from Andalucía and Murcia received free one-way train tickets and temporary free accommodation on arrival. Many Catalans believe that the purpose of this government-subsidized migration was not only to provide a labor force for booming

Catalan industries but also to break the back of the Catalan language. Today, many of the people who came to Catalonia at that time and have been living there for twenty or thirty years still do not speak a word of Catalan. Their children, who went to school in Catalonia, can probably speak it correctly, but they do not. This Catalan-resistant segment of the population is a source of great irritation to many Catalans, and it is because of them that foreigners find themselves pressured to speak Catalan once they are judged to have been around long enough to learn it.

Many Americans in Catalonia resist learning Catalan, either because they are afraid it will interfere with their learning of Castilian or because they simply do not want to put effort into learning Catalan when they will never have a chance to use it outside of Catalonia. Resisting Catalan or Euskera or Gallego will not endear Americans to the people of those regions of Spain, while learning a little of any of those languages will be very well received. Catchphrases and expressions are easy to learn and will help bridge the gap.

Nonverbal Communication

Appearance

Appearance is important in Spain, as it is in most of Europe. Sociologists Amando de Miguel and Marta Escuin[1] link Spanish concern with appearance to life as theater. The Spanish public lifestyle is based on seeing and being seen—at movies, cafés, restaurants, or simply during a *paseo* (stroll).

Categories of clothing in Spain are similar to those in the United States: formal wear for special events; business attire; and more casual styles for weekends. However, there are noticeable differences. Formal wear is not as extreme; for example, at a wedding Spanish men wear dark suits rather than tuxedos, and women wear tailored suits or dresses rather than brightly colored gowns. Business dress codes are stricter in Spain, with suits and ties the norm for men in white-collar environments. "Dress-down Fridays" are virtually unknown. Spaniards do dress more casually on weekends, but they are still more careful dressers than are Americans. Only the clothing of teenagers and vacationers is as relaxed as American casual wear.

Spanish color choices are generally more subdued, though Spanish women of all ages wear more jewelry and often more makeup than American women. Fashion is more closely followed than in the United States, but at the same time women and men have a basic wardrobe of good-quality tailored clothing. Factory outlets and consignment stores are unknown.

Americans know that dress can be important in social and career settings, but this conflicts with the value they place on comfort, practicality, and egalitarianism. They think that when not obliged to dress up, one should dress down. Therefore, many Americans are irritated that Spaniards value appearance over comfort and practicality, while Spaniards often urge their American friends to make more of their appearance.

Formality and Informality

Americans are more informal in communicating with one another than are members of most other cultures, including Spain. This informality, which manifests itself as "friendliness," is due to the principle of egalitarianism, which is a strong value among Americans. Outward friendliness is expected, and the absence of it may be construed as tenseness, standoffishness, or hostility. Spaniards, like members of many older and more traditional societies, are much less likely to believe in equality between people. The range of communication in Spain from formal to informal is much greater than in the United States and is determined by the situation, with strangers typically receiving the least "friendly" treatment. This strong contrast between Spaniards and Americans can lead to misunderstandings.

In Spain times have changed in recent years as far as formality is concerned. For example, the polite *usted* (you) form of address has given way in many situations to the familiar *tú*. Clothing styles, manners, and behavior all reflect a liberalization of the earlier formality. However, manners in general are still not as free and easy as in the United States.

Friendliness and Public Seriousness

Spaniards who go to the United States are struck by the friendliness of Americans. One Catalan who moved to the U.S. complained that his face hurt from having to smile so much. The image of the United States projected in Spain through movies and television series does not generally include friendliness, so whatever else Spaniards (who are used to American cops-and-robbers shows and intrigue-ridden family sagas) expect, they do not anticipate that Americans will be personable and friendly. In fact, this characteristic is probably responsible for more 180-degree turns in the attitudes of visiting Spaniards than any other.

In Spain, in contrast, public decorum implies seriousness. Except at fiesta time, people tend to go about without smiles on their faces. Don Quixote was known as the Knight of the Sad Countenance, and in the days of the greatness of Spain's colonial empire, King Philip II set the style of sober black clothes with a plain white ruff around the neck and an unsmiling face. Spaniards at that time were known all over Europe for their serious demeanor.

Americans, especially if they do not speak Spanish well, tend to be put off by unsmiling Spaniards. An American salesman on vacation in Spain, bothered by the sober faces he saw around him, started smiling at strangers to see what would happen and got in return reactions ranging from puzzlement to embarrassment, though he did get at least a few pleased grins.

Outward expression, however, does not necessarily reflect thoughts and feelings, particularly with Spaniards. One

American who discovered this was a young woman traveling alone by air with a toddler and a baby. The baby was supposed to have a ticket although she was traveling on her mother's lap, and at the departure gate the airport officials, finding that the baby's ticket was missing, made the mother wait until they could find a representative of the airline to sort the problem out. Communication between them was by gestures, since neither side spoke the other's language. The American woman, reading only dour faces, assumed that she would be forced to miss her flight and burst into tears. The Spanish officials, upset by the sight of a weeping woman with a baby (the ultimate heart melter), redoubled their search for the airline representative, but it did not occur to them that a smile would be reassuring. Luckily an interpreter was able to tell the American what the Spaniards were saying: "Tell her not to cry; everything will be OK; we won't let the plane go without her." Finally the airline representative arrived and solved the problem, by which time the officials were goo-gooing at the baby, playing with the toddler, and helping the mother carry her luggage onto the plane.

Strangers versus People You Know

The Spanish treatment of strangers is something to which all foreigners, and particularly Americans, have to adjust. "Service with a smile" is an American concept. Spaniards love it when they go to the United States, not just for the smile but for what it implies: that strangers are entitled to the best service. Americans believe that they are entitled to polite and helpful treatment from public servants. This is in sharp contrast to what they will encounter in Spain, except in the hospitality industry. The result is that when Americans are dealing with the Spanish bureaucracy or seeking information or service from Spaniards, there may be serious misunderstandings. The American, who may be feeling confused and stressed, wants the Spaniard to be friendly and helpful. The Spaniard, unsmiling, barks out the minimum of information at high speed. But Americans who react negatively simply assure themselves of even worse treatment the next time. The best response is to remain courteous and patient, which will help make the next interaction more pleasant. In Spain a stranger is no longer a stranger after the first encounter. From then on the relationship is *Ya nos conocemos* (We know each other), and treatment is different.

For many Americans, their first important interaction with the Spanish bureaucracy is in obtaining visas and residency and work permits. The process involves standing in line at many offices and obtaining documents with all sorts of stamps and seals on them, meanwhile never being sure whether everything is in order because nobody provides a comprehensive list of what is required. Frustration is guaranteed. However, time and again Americans find that the person who met them the first time with a set face, brusque answers, and the most unhelpful manner possible treats them on ensuing occasions with cooperation and helpfulness—if the Americans were polite and patient the first time around.

This pattern even extends to Spanish consulates in the United States. An American man went to a consulate to obtain a visa for his wife and was turned away because she did not make the visa petition in person. Well trained after living in Spain for over a year, he remained calm and was polite. Two weeks later he returned to the consulate to apply for a permit to take his dog to Spain (his wife planned to go a few days later for her visa). Not only did he get the permit for the dog, he also got the visa for his wife. Because someone at the consulate knew him, he was no longer a member of the anonymous public but a nice person with a problem.

Body Language
Spanish social relationships usually involve a great deal more bodily contact than those in the United States. The handshake is obligatory at the beginning and end of every conver-

sation with an acquaintance. A conversation between strangers, such as in an information-giving situation (travel agency, bank, public office, etc.), may begin without a handshake, but it will usually end with one; and once the relationship is established, a handshake will begin and end every encounter.

Americans in Spain find themselves shaking hands more often than they do at home, and it takes a while before they learn to offer their hands automatically. This difference between American and Spanish custom was experienced by a Spanish lawyer who worked for an organization with many American employees. After some weeks on the job the lawyer was asked by his American supervisor how things were going. "Not so well," was his reply. "I don't think your Americans trust me. They walk into my office, sit down, ask me whatever questions they have, and then they stand up, say thanks and leave. They never shake hands. I feel like a pariah." The lawyer was mystified when his boss laughed, until he was informed that Americans don't shake hands every time they enter or leave the office of someone they already know. After that he varied his approach, shaking hands with Spaniards and keeping his hands by his sides when visiting with Americans.

Spanish greetings also often include hugs and kisses. Men who are good friends usually greet each other with a hug, and men who are members of the same family often kiss each other on the cheek as well. Women and girls are always greeted by friends and family with a kiss on each cheek. When children or young teenagers are introduced to older people, they usually offer their cheek for a kiss. This can be surprising, especially for a young American male who is introduced to a quite grown-up-looking Spanish teenage girl and finds to his amazement that they are already "on kissing terms."

Even when closing letters the Spanish are affectionate. The normal ending when the correspondents know each other fairly well is *Un abrazo* (a hug), where an American would write "Cordially" or at most "Warm regards." With good friends, men write "Un abrazo" while women often write *Besos* (Kisses).

The question of when to shake hands, when to hug, and when to kiss can be confusing to an outsider. The best procedure for Americans, for whom all this bodily contact is generally quite alien, is to take their cues from the Spaniards they meet and be ready for hugs and kisses as well as handshakes.

Americans touch friends and acquaintances less than Spaniards do, and they avoid touching strangers if at all possible. When accidental contact occurs, they hastily apologize and move away. Americans in Spain have trouble in this regard. One American woman, who lived in Washington, DC, before moving to Spain, said that within the first weeks she had bumped into more strangers (followed by the urge to punch them out) than in all her years in DC. Other Americans have experienced the same annoyance, accompanied by feelings of embarrassment.

Spaniards moving among strangers in public are not preoccupied with keeping out of one another's way. They are thinking about themselves and not about the other people on the street. Therefore, they may quite often stop dead, change direction, or stand in a group on the sidewalk. All of these actions are likely to obstruct the free movement of others. Americans are not expecting people to do any of these things, since they assume that, like themselves, everyone at all times is concerned with keeping out of other people's way. Therefore, when someone stops suddenly or changes direction, the American tends to run right into that person. The American is typically much more upset about this than the Spaniard, who does not share the same taboo about touching strangers. The American feels embarrassed, frustrated, and/or angry. But the Spaniard is breaking American rules, not Spanish rules. If someone stops in front of Spaniards or stands with a group blocking the sidewalk, Spaniards simply touch that person on the back or shoulder and the person then moves out of the way. In Spain, the way to move through a crowd is by touching people. When this happens to Americans, they feel that they are being shoved or jostled, which is such taboo behavior in the United States that Americans react with anger, like the woman who found herself wanting to punch people out. This seems to be one of the differences that takes quite a while to get used to. Americans who have been in Spain for years and have adapted in other ways to cultural differences still complain about Spanish crowd behavior. But at least they no longer feel the urge to hit people.

One thing that would seem too trivial to mention, if it were not so frequently noted by Americans, is the smell of garlic on Spaniards' breath. Garlic is an omnipresent condiment in Spanish cuisine. *Allioli* (garlic mayonnaise) is one of the great Catalan inventions and is extremely pungent, as are many Spanish dishes. People may therefore smell of garlic, especially after lunch. One American woman said that it was a year before she realized that the "terrible" odor she so often smelled in Spain was in fact the innocuous odor of garlic; and, worse, that she herself undoubtedly smelled the same, since she had joyfully taken to eating some of the most pungent of Spanish dishes. Some Spanish men may also smell of wine or brandy after lunch. As ethnic cuisines have gained a stronger foothold in the United States, the perfume of garlic has become more familiar to Americans, so it may no longer come as such a shock in Spain. In any case, Spaniards are fastidious about personal hygiene and typically also smell of soap and/or cologne.

Communication Styles

Greetings and Farewells
Spaniards are much more punctilious about greetings and farewells than are Americans. In addition to the handshakes, kisses, and hugs normal among friends and acquaintances,

Spaniards feel obligated to at least murmur a greeting whenever entering a space where there are other people. Whether
it be an elevator, an office, a waiting room, or a store, Spaniards always say "Hola" ("Hello") or "Buenos días/Buenas
tardes" ("Good morning/Good afternoon"), getting a general
murmured response. When leaving, they say Adiós (Good-
bye). It takes Americans some time to learn to do this, accustomed as they are to entering and leaving places unan-
nounced—which in Spain is considered rude behavior.

Another little quirk of Spanish greeting customs is that if
they meet someone on the street and are going to stop and
have a conversation, they say Hola, but if they are simply
going to pass each other, they say Adiós. While it seems a
little strange to say good-bye when you first see someone,
Adiós can also be translated as "Go with God," which makes
the custom a little more comprehensible.

Conversation
A typical comment that both Spaniards and Americans make
about one another is "They're so loud." Americans are usually reacting to Spanish decibel levels in social situations,
where Spaniards are unquestionably loud. Signs in bars and
restaurants in Andalucía warning Prohibido cantar (No singing) may seem strange until the first time one hears a group
of Spaniards singing; even if unaccompanied by hand clap-
ping, it is deafening. The signs outside bars and nightclubs
that read "Respeten el descanso de los vecinos" are trying to
counteract the tendency of noisy groups to hang out in the
street, hablando fuerte (talking loudly), as the Spaniards say
disarmingly. Americans would call it yelling. One American
who had lived in Spain for five years commented that his first
ride in a train crowded with teenagers left him exhausted
from the noise. Some time later, he was sitting on the same
train in the same circumstances. The noise and confusion
were the same, but he placidly read his book and talked to his
neighbors and looked out of the window, oblivious to the

racket. Similarly, Americans who have grown accustomed to Spain have learned to block out the noise in bars and restaurants and carry on their own conversations. Spaniards, on the other hand, wince at American loud voices in public. American tourists in groups, reacting enthusiastically to the sights around them, are extremely noticeable on Spanish streets and public transportation because Spaniards in these situations tend to be quiet.

Another thing that Americans find different about Spanish conversation style is long-windedness. Americans often comment that it takes Spaniards a long time and a lot of words to say anything. If the American is in a hurry or feeling frustrated, this long-windedness seems like wasting time or beating around the bush. The American urge to get to the point differs greatly from the Spanish tendency to cover all possible bases and follow up on every idea. Spaniards generally admire American conciseness both in speech and in writing, but they emulate it only if they have worked for or with Americans. Most people in Spain talk more and longer about things than Americans consider necessary, but the longer they live in Spain, the more tolerant Americans become. Newcomers would be wise to try to learn to strike a balance between American conciseness and Spanish prolixity.

Coexisting with long-windedness is a Spanish tendency to be hasty in conversation, jumping to positive or negative conclusions. For example, when asked a question or faced with a problem, a Spaniard may answer before hearing the speaker out. Similarly, a Spaniard may say "We'll do this or that" before considering other factors that will cause that decision to be changed or reversed. Americans find this trait annoying, since they would prefer to get the right information the first time. They learn to be patient and persistent to ensure that the matter has been fully discussed and the conclusion is the right one.

Finally, Americans learn not to take Spaniards literally. Spaniards tend toward exaggeration, which can be disconcerting to literal-minded Americans. Also, what Spaniards say and what they mean can be two different things. For example, "The document is ready and you can come to pick it up" may really mean "The document will be ready once it has been signed, and I assume it will have been signed by the time you get here."

Avoidance of Confrontation

One major difference often pointed out between Americans and Spaniards is that Americans are much more ready to engage in direct confrontation than are Spaniards. American teachers in Spain often find that the expression of strong opinions frequently goes unchallenged. Americans tend to attribute this to passivity, backward thinking, or lack of awareness on the part of the students. Similarly, American managers often find that their Spanish subordinates will not confront them directly, though the Spaniards may have strong feelings which they later express to coworkers. Silence to Americans generally means consent, because they expect someone who disagrees with something to speak up and say so. Americans are taught that it is their right to dissent and disagree. Spaniards are likely, especially in a group, to keep quiet if someone says something with which they don't agree. Spaniards generally consider direct confrontation impolite. To contradict someone, especially in front of other people, is a challenge that may be met with anger. It is perhaps significant that the word *discusión* in Spanish means "argument." Americans should not encourage the open expression of different views unless they want to referee a shouting match. Neither should they interpret silence to meant consent. If they want to know what Spaniards really think, an open meeting may not be the place to find out.

A useful concept for Americans is that of high-context versus low-context communication. In the case of a meeting, for example, context refers to who is present, who is absent, events leading up to the meeting, who is running it, where people are sitting, and body language as well as the actual words spoken. Typically, Americans are low-context, meaning that they give most importance to the words, while Spaniards are high-context, meaning that the context is at least as important as the words, if not more so.

Speaking English

Studying English has been the rage in Spain since the mid-1970s. There are any number of small language schools offering classes in English, as well as highly successful television series and self-study courses sold in installments. English is now the primary foreign language taught in Spanish schools, and the national and regional governments have spent considerable sums on retraining teachers, equipping schools, and designing new curricula. The results are variable, but in general, Spanish young people are learning English to an impressive standard.

Among people over forty the situation is more complicated. They went to school at a time when French was more commonly taught than English, so if they have learned English it has been since leaving high school, by going to a private academy or taking courses abroad. Those who have been exposed to English through their professional activities may know it very well, while there may be others who at age fifty have never had a chance to learn any at all.

At any rate, there is no doubt that knowledge of English is one of the keys to professional advancement in Spain. A glance at the advertisements for professional positions in the Sunday papers will show that almost every opening requires knowledge of English. Older executives who are already established may be able to make it through the rest of their careers without English, but junior and midlevel people realize that not knowing English will place serious limitations on future advancement.

This situation gives rise quite frequently to another manifestation of the pícaro: the desperate executives who show up at language schools demanding the most intensive English course available. Having managed to get a job by claiming to know English, they now need to learn some as fast as possible before getting caught. One can imagine the reaction of an American boss on finding out that a new employee has mis-represented his or her knowledge of English and that nobody in the hiring process caught it.

In a multinational corporation the top-ranking Spanish personnel will usually be fluent in English, but few Americans can speak Spanish well. Two problems may arise in this circumstance; the first is a double standard regarding language learning. The Spanish executives' jobs depend to some extent on their knowledge of English. It was a prerequisite to their being hired, and they may still be taking classes in their off-hours. Meanwhile, there may be American executives in the same organization who either cannot speak Spanish at all or speak it badly and make no effort to improve. The signifi-cance of the double standard does not escape Spaniards who, by and large, resent it.

The second problem is that an English-only office envi-ronment interferes with the Americans' cross-cultural adap-tation. If the Spaniards who work closely with Americans speak fluent American-accented English, they may often seem like pseudo-Americans. If, in addition, office systems are replicas of the U.S. home office, Americans may forget that they are operating in Spain, not back home in Ohio, and will have more difficulty dealing with the Spanish environment outside the office and its influence on office events. Even if the American's Castilian is limited and major business still has to be done in English or through a translator, an attempt to compromise between English and Castilian in the running of the office is an investment, not only in a better office atmosphere, but in smoother adaptation to living and work-ing in Spain.

---

[1] Amando De Miguel, and Marta Escuin, *ABC de la opinión española*. Madrid: Espasa Calpe, 1997.

Encounter Four: Ya Me lo Pagará Mañana

Michael goes to the neighborhood bakery early one Saturday morning and chooses two loaves of bread and some pastries. Reaching into his pocket, he finds that he has no change, only a single large bill. The shopkeeper is also short of change and hands him the bread and the cash register receipt, saying, "Ya me lo pagará mañana."

Michael should

A. wait to pay until his next weekly shopping trip.

B. find a way to break his large bill, get some change, and pay within the hour.

C. make a point of paying within the next day or two.

D. forget about paying, since the shopkeeper obviously considers the amount trivial.

A. *This option is acceptable—just. A week is a long time to wait before paying.*

B. *Paying within the hour is not necessary. If Michael comes back to pay immediately, people will protest that he should not have bothered but at the same time they will characterize him as particularly polite and thoughtful.*

C. *This is the option that Spaniards would choose.*

D. *Not paying at all is definitely wrong. The shopkeeper does not regard as trivial either the amount of money or the confianza shown in giving Michael credit. Failing to pay will make him a "marked man" in the neighborhood.*

5

Work

High-ranking Americans in multinational corporations or the Foreign Service are somewhat protected from experiencing the differences between Spaniards and Americans in the workplace. Their offices in Spain run to some extent on American home-office rules, and Spanish executives and senior staff have been selected because of their knowledge of American English, their experience in international business and in the United States, and their familiarity with sophisticated modern business practices which are similar across national boundaries.

However, not every American working in Spain is with a multinational corporation or in a position of authority. Many have Spanish supervisors. A musician or dancer has artistic and financial directors; a sports coach has senior coaches or managers; a language teacher has school supervisors and/or directors; a university professor has department heads; and consultants have to deal with the organizations that hired them. These Americans encounter differences in the workplace head-on. Even those employed in multinationals or in purely American organizations such as the Foreign Service or the military come up against the work styles of Spanish staff (canteen workers, chauffeurs, cleaners, white-collar workers)

who are probably "more Spanish" in their attitudes and behaviors than the English-speaking executives and counterparts they interact with most of the time.

Attitudes toward Work

Work Ethic
When asked about the difference between living in Spain
and living in the United States, both Americans and Spaniards are likely to mention the work ethic almost immediately. Americans who have settled in Spain generally say, "I
don't have to work as hard here as I would back home."
Spaniards who have visited or lived in the United States
comment on how hard everyone works. In other words,
Americans "live to work," and Spaniards "work to live." In
the United States work is central to people's lives, and they
tend to devote all their energies to their jobs, at least from
Monday to Friday, often working overtime or skipping lunch.
Many Americans bring work home or go in to the office on
weekends. Working hard is valued, both because work is a
highly esteemed activity and because it is a sign of ambition
and wanting to better oneself, which is also valued. Through
work one pursues achievement, which among Americans is a
significant source of identity and a measure of status. Added
to these traditional values is the increased pressure of work in
the United States. Corporate downsizing, a competitive labor
market, and the pace of change mean that most American
workers are coping with a heavier workload and greater job
insecurity than was the case in earlier decades.

For Spaniards, work is a way of earning a living. Most
people put in their hours on the job but do not work extra
hours except in the case of some ghastly crisis. Skipping
lunch is virtually unheard-of. Once away from work they
switch off completely until they walk back into the office
again. This is one of the reasons Spanish friends sometimes
do not know about one another's jobs, because talking about

work is not a normal part of social life. If there were a severe problem at work that was causing personal difficulties, one might discuss it with family or intimate friends but rarely with acquaintances or in casual conversation.

Many Americans expect people in Latin countries, Spain included, to be slow-moving and easygoing, taking siestas all the time and saying mañana whenever asked to do anything. The only parts of Spain that bear any relation to this image are the Canary Islands and Andalucía. The further north one goes, the more intense the work ethic becomes. The Basques and Catalans are famous in Spain for their industriousness and acquisitive instinct. Big-city professionals (with whom Americans are most likely to come into contact) work extremely hard, just like their counterparts in the United States. Furthermore, Spaniards often have two jobs or combine work and study.

However, most Spaniards do not want to look driven. Workaholism is not fashionable in Spain; indeed, Spaniards consider it to be rather unattractive. The Spanish style is to take a relaxed attitude toward work and to separate it clearly from one's personal life. Spaniards often see Americans as being rather boring work machines who do not know how to balance their priorities and make time in their lives for fun (see chapter 6). Spaniards often say to Americans in Spain, "You like it better here, don't you? Life is pleasanter here, isn't it?"

Some Spaniards feel that the long Spanish working day leads to a more relaxed attitude toward work (typical office hours are 9:00 to 1:30 or 2:00 and 4:00 to 7:00). Whatever the reason, Spaniards certainly work at a more relaxed pace than Americans and expect to have time during a normal workday to catch up on the personal news of their coworkers, look at the paper, enjoy a coffee break, take their full two-hour lunch, and maybe run a personal errand. Americans may find this disconcerting, but on the other hand American managers in Spain find absenteeism very low. Where an

American worker needing to transact personal business might take a sick day, a Spanish worker would probably just take a few hours off, because leaving work for personal business is accepted.

In the summer most offices in Spain change to *horario de verano*, or summer schedule, which usually means a six-hour workday during July and August, though some organizations start summer hours in June and do not end them until early September. The reason for this change in schedule becomes clear after you have lived in Spain awhile. First, everything slows down because of the number of people who are on vacation. The impact on business of summer vacations is greater in Spain than in the United States because all employees are entitled to a month's paid vacation, and most vacations are taken in either July or August. Second, the summer is very hot. Even air-conditioned offices cannot alleviate the searing heat of a Spanish afternoon in July or August, when the only reasonable thing for civilized human beings to do is to sleep in a room with all the shades pulled down. Because of this, Spaniards work without a break from about 9:00 to about 3:00 and then stop for the rest of the day. They cannot believe that in the United States, despite summer temperatures in excess of one hundred degrees Fahrenheit in some places, Americans make no concessions to the heat—except to work in air-conditioned offices.

What is interesting about the summer schedule, which much more closely resembles the American working day, is that Spaniards typically work more steadily and in a more concentrated fashion during these six hours than during the two sessions of their normal working day the rest of the year. Many Spaniards prefer their summer schedule, not just because the total number of hours is shorter but also because it means they can get work over with and still have some of the day left. This seems to confirm the theory that the length of the Spanish working day contributes in part to the Spanish attitude toward work. Despite predictions that European

Union membership would bring changes, the Spanish schedule remains the same—one of the most striking ways in which Spain is different.

Americans are often perceived by others, including Spaniards, as self-starters who make their own plans and maintain control over what they do, while Spaniards tend to wait to be directed. If in an office the American is the manager, it is his or her job to initiate and direct; Spaniards will wait for direction because they are subordinates. They may feel that they cannot initiate because it is not their prerogative, and they may also avoid being too self-starting because they do not want to create more work for themselves. Anyone who has worked in the United States is perfectly familiar with coworkers who do not take initiative or are simply not interested in their jobs. But such people are rarely sent on overseas assignments.

Americans sent abroad are likely to be highly motivated and work oriented and will probably find it difficult to get used to the relaxed Spanish style. It is their job to manage and lead, to set an example, and, especially, to live up to home-office expectations. As one American pointed out, if you have been hired as a foreign expert, then you have to *be* a foreign expert.

Nevertheless, some adaptation is desirable, particularly in distinguishing between the goal of getting the work done according to certain standards and the *style* of getting it done; in other words, there is usually more than one way to reach a given goal.

One of the major challenges faced by the American manager in Spain is to find ways to achieve the organization's goals by incorporating Spanish culture-based work styles rather than trying to replace them with the American work ethic.

Ambition and Success
Spaniards see Americans as highly ambitious, restless people who are never content with what they have and will sell their

homes and move across the country or switch to a completely different profession in order to satisfy those ambitions. This is not common in Spain. Spaniards say, *"Somos comodones"* ("We like things easy") and will not take the risks involved in making these changes. Americans view this attitude as lackadaisical, which may be in part because success for an American is highly personal and defined by the visible rewards of one's own efforts. For Spaniards success is more a matter of status, either social status or that conferred by position. A Spaniard might be impressed by a person with the title of *catedrático* (tenured professor), while an American might be more concerned with the size of the professor's salary, the number of his or her publications, and the offices held in prestigious organizations. Similarly, a Spaniard might have a hard time understanding how an American could give up a position with the title of president or director because the salary was insufficient or the work unchallenging.

For a Spaniard, success lies in the title as much as in the salary, and much more than in the work. This may be another reason why Spaniards have traditionally been loath to change jobs. The attractions of a better salary or more interesting work are outweighed by the disadvantages of having to start again and lose the status one has already achieved. Spaniards would generally rather stay in one job and wait for the promotion that will eventually arrive because of seniority. Americans are shocked when they attempt to motivate Spaniards by appealing to their ambition and find that, at least in the American sense, it is missing.

Discipline and Supervision

Work in Spain is governed by a formal regulatory and disciplinary structure to a much greater extent than in the United States. All employees are covered by the *Estatuto del trabajador* (workers' code), which sets out the requirements for proper job performance, including punctuality, industriousness, working relationships, loyalty to the employer, and so on.

Breach of this code can lead to disciplinary action in the form of written admonitions, warnings, suspensions, docked pay, and even dismissal. Many organizations have a *Comité de empresa* (employees' council), the function of which is to inform, counsel, and defend the employees but also to warn them in the case of breach of the workers' code. At the same time, trade unions are active and powerful in Spain, as they are all over Europe. Americans are usually astounded at the level of job security in Spain and the difficulty of firing a worker.

Americans supervising Spaniards may find themselves at a loss. An American who coached a volleyball team in Murcia commented that Spanish players would fool around at the beginning of practice rather than getting down to drills right away. She was also shocked that her players let emotions interfere with their game, deliberately playing badly if they were angry with the coach or the referee, for example. Finally, she complained about players showing up late not only for practice but also for matches and tournaments.

For Americans, these behaviors (lack of dedication, insufficient emotional control, and failure to be punctual) demonstrate a lack of self-discipline. Americans assume that people will discipline themselves in order to achieve an objective, but Spaniards do not function that way. Whatever their objectives, they do not lose sight of or subordinate their personal feelings and inclinations. If they are tired, angry, or upset, they show it; and punctuality, while desirable, is not such an absolute value as in the United States.

In an American work environment, if interpersonal difficulties arise the manager can assume that they will be aired and resolved, perhaps with the assistance of the human resources department. If a solution is not reached, one of the employees may leave, or the manager may terminate a "problem" person within the bounds of employment law and union regulations. However, the situation is more delicate in Spain. Spaniards may express their feelings more strongly than would be acceptable in most U.S. workplaces; for example, refusing to speak to a coworker following a disagreement. But airing the problem may not lead to a solution, and termination is probably not an option.

In dealing with such challenges, American managers need to be cautious. They should concentrate initially on building relationships and finding out where interpersonal fault lines are. Even if they are comfortable in a counseling and mediation role in the United States, they should not assume that Spaniards will react to such approaches as Americans would. It may be safer for American managers to use low context as a shield, focusing their attention on desired results and avoiding comment on people's behavior. Above all, they should not attempt to threaten or intimidate, since Spaniards can be both rebellious and vengeful.

Teamwork

While Spaniards and Americans do not approach teamwork in exactly the same way, the differences between them are perhaps mostly a matter of opinion, especially in contrast to other cultures, such as Japan, where there is a strong orientation toward team spirit and a collective mentality.

Some would say that Spaniards work poorly in teams. It has been remarked that Santiago Ramón y Cajal, the Spanish scientist who won the Nobel Prize for his work in endocrinology, achieved this award for work done mainly alone, without the need for a research team or a complicated support system. The implication here is that the Nobel Prize could not be won by Spaniards in a team, only by one Spaniard alone. In an article in *El País* entitled "Why Spaniards Innovate So Little," Eduardo Punset, an economist and an economics and political writer, identified teamwork as one of the prerequisites for innovation among people of like minds and like interests—something he felt to be lacking, if not in Spaniards, at least in the Spanish educational system.[1] The American volleyball coach previously mentioned found teamwork, as she expected it from her American perspective, clearly lacking in her Spanish teams.

On the other hand, Spaniards do work in teams under some circumstances. It is common, for instance, in Spanish schools and universities for students to present projects, papers, and theses that are the work of a group rather than an individual. At conferences where both Spaniards and foreigners are giving presentations, it is interesting to see how many of the Spanish presentations are the work of a team, while the other presentations are usually the work of individuals.

Perhaps the major difference between Spain and the United States in this respect is that teamwork is actively fostered by American supervisors and managers. In the United States the tradition of clubs and associations as well as the national love of sports and the emphasis on sports in school imbue Americans with a belief in the value of teamwork. This value often coexists, however, with a strong individualistic, competitive drive.

The analogy of the "winning team" is used by American managers to define optimum work relationships. Writers on business and organizational behavior suggest that one of the most prominent elements contributing to the success of the best companies is that the employees think of themselves as a team and cooperate actively with one another to achieve team goals, whether related to manufacturing, customer service, sales, or another function of the company. Techniques used in training and development, such as Outward Bound programs in which participants learn to trust and depend on the other members of the group, are also based on "winning team" assumptions.

Though Spanish work colleagues think of themselves as members of a family, teamwork does not automatically result. A family consists of people of different ages, degrees of education, political ideas, and personalities, all held together by emotional and blood ties. A team, on the other hand, usually consists of selected people with similar or complementary education, skills, background, and goals. The Spanish relationship of familia at work, like that of the family at home, is to a great extent an emotional one with ties that stem from shared experiences, long acquaintance, personal attachment, and the feeling of being bonded for life.

American managers, teachers, or coaches who come to work in Spain will probably find that team building is needed. Spaniards, for their part, should probably expect American managers to be concerned with teamwork, since this is one of the well-known canons of modern American management style. However, once again, Americans should not attempt simply to transplant ideas wholesale.

Competitiveness
The American belief in individualism goes hand in hand with a strong competitive spirit. The achievements of an individual are valued above the harmony of the group, and individualism and competitiveness are both seen as positive. In Spain, however, both individualism and competitiveness are seen as actually or potentially negative. Significantly, both might be translated as *egoismo* (egotism). Competitiveness, in particular, is associated with envidia, "the Spanish vice."

American bosses should be wary of fostering what they see as "healthy competition," as one American executive found out when he attempted to hire someone for the newly created position of controller in the Spanish branch of a growing multinational company. Wanting to fill the job from inside, the American identified three people as likely candidates. He then decided to observe each of them for six months, evaluate their performance over that period, and only then make the appointment. He next called in each of the three, told them of the availability of the job, and informed them of his plans. So far, so good. But he then also told each of them who the other two candidates were and that they were in open competition. That was his mistake.

Earlier, his secretary had tried in vain to persuade him not to declare the competition open. "No, no," said the American, "that's the way I would do it in the States and that's the way I'm going to do it here. They'll work harder and show their best." Unfortunately, the results were not what he expected. One of the candidates, the best of the three, resigned on the spot, saying that he refused to be a part of what was going to happen. The other two candidates tore each other to shreds, using every possible stratagem to strengthen their own positions and weaken the competitor's. At the end of six months, one of them was appointed controller and the other promptly resigned. Thus the company lost two out of three good people and suffered the consequences of open warfare carried out over the fateful period. It is to the credit of the CEO that he privately admitted his error, but the damage had already been done.

The moral of this story is that competition is not the same for a Spaniard as for an American. For Americans it is generally assumed to be positive, healthy, and a normal part of working life. For Spaniards, it is often negative and destructive and an invitation to *envidia*. Americans should be wary of using individual competition to motivate people, both inside the organization and out.

Growth

U.S. business publications devote a lot of attention to mergers, ambitious expansion plans, initial public offerings, and other forms of rapid growth and change. This phenomenon is not restricted to major corporations but is a feature of business life for even small or midsized organizations. American businesspeople are constantly watching the competition and are convinced of the need to grow and change in order to survive. Financial institutions encourage such ambitions in businesses, as in individuals, by making credit available for growth.

Growth and change are equally important to major Spanish corporations increasing their activities beyond Spain's borders. However, a person who is carrying on a centuries-old family concern, whether hotel, restaurant, vineyard, or factory, is also admired in Spain. Spaniards are just as impressed by a business that has been in operation for a hundred years and hasn't changed appreciably as by one that was started only a few years back and has performed spectacularly.

Many companies and organizations in Spain are not only small but are also run by families. Staff may consist entirely of family members or employees who have been around so long they have come to be regarded as family. This stability is antithetical to radical change or rapid growth. Entry into the European Union presented Spain with the opportunity of a lifetime for growth, change, and modernization. National and local governments and, to a lesser extent, chambers of commerce and trade organizations took it upon themselves to set goals for Spanish business. On the one hand, it was feared that Spanish business and agriculture were relatively unprepared to deal with competition from the rest of Europe as protectionist trade barriers came down. On the other hand, international investors (including the United States) saw the opportunity in Spain for high growth and, with it, high return on investment. An influx of investment capital and the expanded market represented by the E.U. and its trading partners combined gave the Spanish economy spectacular growth rates in the decade following Spain's integration into Europe.

Ethics and Corruption
The week's headlines in any major Spanish newspaper usually reveal some kind of scandal involving alleged ethical lapses in prominent business or political figures.

One sort of scandal involves defective or falsely labeled merchandise. Over the years such scandals have ranged from adulterated cooking oil to defective aluminum used in construction. Consumer advocacy has historically been much weaker in Spain than in the United States, but greater prosperity and membership in the European Union have brought higher standards, a stricter regulatory environment, and increased public expectation of quality in consumer products.

Another type of scandal focuses on illegal activity, misappropriation of funds, and too-cozy relationships between business and government. Conflicts of interest arise in Spain as in the United States whenever established relationships exist. However, in the U.S. the public's right to know is a far stronger tradition than in Spain. Since the transition to democracy, there has been more disclosure and transparency in Spain, but government secrecy and individual privacy are still more protected than in the U.S. In both countries the party in opposition is the most likely to level attacks against the government.

Work Environment

Hierarchy

Americans interviewed for this book generally said that they found Spaniards more conscious of hierarchy than Americans. Spaniards said that most Americans seemed less status-conscious than Spaniards. It may be that these Spaniards were simply reacting to the friendly, up-front image projected by many Americans and that this friendliness obscures the fact that Americans are in fact quite status-conscious, though in ways different from the Spanish.

In any event it appears that the source of status differs between the two countries. While for Americans it is based on achievement and material possessions, for Spaniards it is related much more to position, title, and public image. Pride and honor have been recurrent themes in Spanish literature. Foreigners, from respected historians to popular novelists and commentators such as James Michener, have often taken note of the importance of pride in the Spanish psyche. Some historians trace it back to the reconquest and the preoccupation with being *hidalgo*, that is, "somebody" (literally, the son of somebody). It is probably questionable whether a modern Spanish man working in a multinational corporation is preoccupied with being an hidalgo, but he undoubtedly has a clear idea of who he is and what is due him according to his status.

Putting oneself in the Spaniard's place may help Americans to be more tactful than one high-level American manager whose corporation had offices in both Barcelona and Madrid. This manager visited the Barcelona office and then, to save time, had Barcelona set up interviews with various influential businesspeople and public figures in Madrid. He thus bypassed completely the head of the Madrid office (the most senior person in the corporate hierarchy) who, on hearing of the scheduled interviews from the people who had been contacted, summarily canceled them. The visitor's behavior was very American in placing speed and convenience over considerations of hierarchy; the Madrid boss's reaction was very Spanish in placing personal honor and considerations of hierarchy over efficiency.

Authority and Respect

What is particularly striking about the preceding anecdote is that it contrasts sharply with a normally ingrained respect for authority in Spain. Politeness is often defined in terms of respect; to be rude in Castilian is *faltar al respeto* (literally, to be lacking in respect). Spaniards are brought up to respect people who are older or in authority. In turn, they expect respect from those who they feel owe it to them. This system of respect is by no means as strong as in Japan or some Arab cultures, but it is certainly stronger than in the United States, where one of the basic tenets of the culture is social equality and where being overly respectful still carries a connotation of inequality. Americans are usually very conscious of their rights as individuals; they are quick to speak up in meetings and make their opinions heard, or readily approach people in authority to talk about things that are bothering them. Americans discuss problems with their supervisors or express discontent with levels of pay, working conditions, or anything else that is not to their liking. Spaniards are not so quick to do this, perhaps because of respect or because of cynicism about the results that are likely to be achieved.

Americans in a work situation with Spaniards notice that they are less likely to speak up in meetings, write petitions or letters, or solicit interviews in which to talk over problems. Seeing this, Americans may assume—wrongly—that Spaniards have no opinions, or are unconcerned about public or personal problems, or perhaps are still living with the effects of forty years of dictatorship (or even that the almost forty years of dictatorship were made possible by just such passivity). What is true is that Spaniards are concerned with being subtle and with choosing the right time to speak in order to ensure that they do not make themselves or their colleagues look foolish. Spaniards are in general afraid of looking foolish (*hacer el ridículo*) and will go to a lot of trouble to avoid it. They may prefer to state their opinions in private to the person concerned rather than in an open meeting, or wait and see what time will bring if they remain silent, or perhaps enlist the support of the comité de empresa, a neutral body whose function it is to express their opinions for them.

Business Education
In Spain, as in the United States, the level of formal business education and training is very different between major corporations and small- or medium-sized businesses. Upper-level professionals in corporations are far more likely to have completed specialized studies in business than their counterparts in small businesses.

Excellent management training programs, both full- and part-time, are offered at Spanish universities and private schools, mostly at the graduate level. A wealth of information is available through trade organizations, chambers of commerce, trade shows, and specialized business and technical publications. American best sellers on business topics are quick to appear in Spanish translation.

However, business education and training probably permeate more of the workforce in the United States than in Spain. Americans are far more likely than Spaniards to gain work experience in high school and college and to choose business studies as an undergraduate major. An array of short-term skills training programs are available in the U.S., because of the assumption that constant training is a competitive necessity. In Spain, there is less focus on specialized skills training and more on hands-on work experience.

Work Styles

Rewards and Promotions
Personal goal setting by employees may be found in multinationals, but one would have to look a long time before finding it in most Spanish organizations, large or small. There seem to be two main reasons for this. First, in a hierarchical society with status based on position, subordinates are not often encouraged to think for themselves or to set their own goals, which can be seen as a way of defining and influencing both their roles in the organization and the organization itself. Spanish bosses are often simply too autocratic to allow this type of autonomous thinking in their employees. Secondly, in the United States the practice of personal goal setting is usually tied in with some kind of reward system based on an appraisal of the employee's performance in relation to corporate—and sometimes personal—goals. Rewards in the form of money or promotion for work well done are expected. This assumes, first, that the pay policies of the organization provide

for financial rewards and, second, that the personnel structure provides for promotions. It also implies that organizations need to offer such rewards to valuable employees in order to ensure they are not enticed away by some competing organization.

These three assumptions are probably what make the United States the land of milk and honey in the minds of many Spaniards. In Spain pay structures in businesses resemble those in government, where, because of union activity, raises are often negotiated on a national basis once a year and are strictly tied to status within the organization. Promotions are often determined by seniority or loyalty as much as (or more than) high performance. Further, with the job situation being so tight, employers know that the danger of losing good employees is relatively slim, and the need to provide inducements for them to stay is correspondingly less pressing. Recognizing these conditions may help Americans understand why Spaniards sometimes appear unambitious and not identified with their work.

Decision Making and Problem Solving

The greater consciousness of status and hierarchy in Spain reflects and reinforces a more autocratic management style than Americans are used to. This difference also shows up in problem-solving and decision-making styles. In a Spanish organization the line of authority is likely to be top-down, with the highest person in the hierarchy making the decisions essentially alone. One result is that Spanish managers frequently make a decision and then have to rescind or modify it because of protests or pressures from people affected. Workers may strike or threaten to strike and customers or constituents may raise a hue and cry.

American decision making is top-down too (in contrast, for example, to the Japanese, whose bottom-up, consensus style of decision making is now famous), but American executives are much more inclined to consult, gather other opinions, and test the waters than Spanish executives.

But Americans, for all their friendly ways and easy consul-
tations, surprise Spaniards with their ability to make drastic
decisions with severe effects. They will, for example, close an
unprofitable branch office, putting people out of work, under
circumstances where Spaniards might hesitate. Spaniards are
likely to be influenced by tradition, human factors, or simple
unwillingness to make an unpopular decision.

Planning, Details, and Systems

When President Ronald Reagan visited Madrid in 1985, he
was preceded by the usual advance team whose job it was to
make sure everything had been properly planned and would
run smoothly. An article in *El País* covering preparations for
the president's visit commented on *el prolijo detallismo de los
americanos* (the Americans' unlimited passion for details),
which was driving Spanish counterparts to distraction.

Not long afterward the prime minister of Spain, Felipe
González, made an official visit to China, accompanied by
numerous government officials and prominent businesspeople.
The purpose of the visit was both political and economic, and
it was one of the most significant foreign trips of González's
first administration. To the consternation of the Spaniards
(Chinese reactions were not reported), the government mis-
sion arrived in Beijing some six hours late, causing all the
welcoming ceremonies and the official banquet to be postponed and the schedule for the entire visit to be altered. The
reason: the prime minister's plane had to make an unex-
pected detour. Someone had failed to obtain permission for
the plane to cross the airspace of a Middle Eastern country.
A little *detallismo* would not have been amiss here.

Spaniards think that Americans worry too much about
details, are obsessively pessimistic (saying "What if...?" too
much), and want to have everything nailed down. They also
fuss if anything is late, misplaced, or confused. Americans
think that Spaniards leave far too much to chance, work out

only the general outlines of a plan and none of the details, and don't consider the possibility that something might go wrong.

The American concern with detail is closely allied to the American predilection for systems, with everything clearly labeled and under control. They like information, a lot of it, and they do not like being in doubt or being taken by surprise. One Spaniard being interviewed for this book smiled at the very idea of its being written. "You are writing a handbook," he said, "something dear to the hearts of Americans, full of detailed information that will make things clear and lessen ambiguity and confusion."

While they often admire the results, Spaniards find American *detallismo* unnerving, and if they are expected to display the same attention to detail because of an American boss or rules from American headquarters, it takes considerable adaptation on their part. Americans who have adapted to Spanish ways have come to accept that details may not be attended to, that information may not always be exact, and that they have to loosen up a little and not fuss so much.

Spaniards rely on chance or luck much more than Americans do. While lotteries have increased in popularity in the United States, they can't match Spain, where they are a national addiction. There are half a dozen different lotteries in which people participate on a regular basis. Lottery ticket sellers wander through bars and restaurants carrying sheaves of tickets, and it seems that on every street corner there is a lottery ticket booth. The Spanish also depend on *suerte* (luck) more than Americans do, whether referring to exam results (Americans would think they should have studied harder), finding a hotel room (Americans would think they should have called ahead), or talking their way around a regulation (Americans would think they should take no for an answer).

Trusting to luck is not compatible with thinking that something might go wrong. Americans generally have a contingency plan worked out in case something goes awry so that, when it does, there is an alternative course of action already determined which enables the problem to be solved quickly and painlessly. In Spain there is usually no contingency plan, which means that dealing with problems creates a lot more confusion and emotion. People get tense and start raising their voices. Even a relatively minor hitch, which is usually solvable without too much difficulty, is accompanied in Spain by a chorus of angry words, raised voices, mutterings, and threats which, in the United States, would generally denote a much more serious breakdown in the system. On one occasion at New York's Kennedy Airport, two Spanish executives were waiting at the Iberia desk to have their connecting flights rescheduled because of the delayed arrival of their flight from Spain. The desk was swamped with passengers, some of them irate and all needing to be rescheduled, which was handled by the American staff with quiet efficiency. When his turn came, one of the Spanish executives murmured to the other, "Son apagados, pero van haciendo" ("They're very low-key, but they get on with the job"). He was struck by the absence of fuss in what was potentially an emotional, if not explosive, situation.

On the other hand, Spaniards are concerned that too much planning leads to loss of spontaneity and flexibility. Americans sometimes seem to Spaniards too hung up on their own plans and systems and unable or unwilling to deviate from them in order to solve a problem. Strict and inflexible are adjectives that Spaniards often use about Americans, especially when adherence to a plan or system ignores the personal impact it has on those involved. This excessive commitment to plans and systems is somewhat of a paradox, since Americans tend to pride themselves on their flexibility and are quite willing to change plans if it helps to solve problems. But changes for other reasons are not well received. The more vigorously the Americans pursue their plans and implement their systems, the more the Spaniards push them to be flexible, which in turn causes the Americans to stiffen up and become extremely annoyed at what they consider slapdash Spanish attitudes.

A related issue is the Spanish disregard for danger. Startling to the cautious American, it is most apparent on the road. Spaniards drive much faster and take more risks than do Americans, and the toll of their reckless abandon is reflected, in part, by the terrible statistics of traffic deaths. Americans cite bullfighting as an example of the Spanish cult of death and danger. In the industrial workplace the American preoccupation with protective clothing, heavy shoes, goggles, and head coverings is regarded by many Spaniards as obsessive and pusillanimous. Spaniards prefer to forge ahead, assuming nothing will go wrong. Regrettably, many Americans find this approach so unnerving that their reaction is to reject out of hand things made and done by Spaniards; they refuse treatment by Spanish doctors and dentists and denigrate Spanish workmanship.

Negotiating

Spaniards comment on the American propensity for getting to the point (*ir al grano*). Most Spaniards regard this as a positive attribute in conducting meetings or in writing letters and reports, in contrast with their own tendency to long-windedness. But when an American first encounters a Spaniard, especially in a business negotiation, getting to the point too rapidly can be a hindrance rather than a help. When Spaniards meet someone for the first time to plan, bargain, or negotiate, they want to take the measure of their counterpart and decide whether they would like to do business with him or her. Americans want to know the same thing, but they feel they can accomplish it while discussing the business at hand. The Spaniard would rather get acquainted by discussing world politics or soccer or the beauty of the Pyrenees. Americans are impatient with this type of conversation (which they are inclined to see as beating around the bush or wasting time), but those who do not take the time to get acquainted are likely to appear boorish and abrasive.

Ironically, Americans may leave such an encounter feeling quite satisfied, since Spanish courtesy demands that they follow the lead of the American and, in addition, not show their displeasure. But the Americans in such encounters may have set a trap for themselves that will jeopardize future interaction. James A. McCaffrey and Craig R. Haffner suggest that this kind of behavior constitutes a "false efficiency," since it does not provide for the development of the understanding and trust needed when entering a business relationship.[2] It also results in missed opportunities because of failure to pick up on subtle signals during early encounters.

One example of this false efficiency occurred when a young, eager American executive in a multinational firm called on a potential Spanish client. This client lived in a city about a hundred miles away, and since there were no good air connections, it was arranged that the executive would be chauffeured to the meeting in the company car. On arrival, the driver went off to the men's room and to stretch his legs. When he returned fifteen minutes later, he found the American seated in the car waiting to be driven back. The driver was astounded, and so, no doubt, was the client, who must certainly have expected a wide-ranging discussion lasting one or two hours, probably followed by lunch. No acquaintanceship of any kind could be made in fifteen minutes, and certainly no business matters of any substance could be broached. All the executive seemed to accomplish was to reinforce the image of the time-obsessed American that the Spaniard already had. The driver, of course, regaled the entire company with the story.

The conflict between conciseness and long-windedness does not end once the American and Spanish parties begin discussing the business at hand. Americans usually try to present their information and proposals in a brief, sequential, and neatly packaged form. Spaniards, in contrast, are usually not brief. They discuss things at length, often repeating themselves two or three times. Apparently unrelated information or references are brought in, providing the discussion with more ramifications than Americans are usually ready for.

If disagreement arises during the negotiations, Spaniards are likely to raise their voices. In Spanish conversation, turn taking is less strictly observed than in the United States. Spaniards interrupt speakers without intending offense, and speakers raise their voices in the face of attempted interruption or disagreement. Therefore, Spanish negotiations, like Spanish conversation, can easily become loud. Americans, who value a controlled and dispassionate demeanor in professional situations, are distressed by loud voices, which they interpret as anger, and by interruptions, which they interpret as rudeness.

Disagreement may seem to be anger, both because of the volume and also because Spaniards do not lightly concede points in a discussion or argument. Americans, believing that discussions are sequential, tend to believe that if one is won over to the opposing view, it will be through logic, point by point. However, Spaniards, when faced with opposition, are likely to restate their own point more forcefully, appearing to be categorically rejecting any alternative. Americans should avoid the urge to give up when such obstacles arise. While they may see the negotiation as a road with a series of milestones, the Spaniards see it more as a clearing in the forest. Agreement is often not reached point by point, but rather in general terms once all the factors have been discussed from every angle.

Finally, when agreement is reached, Spaniards often leave details undecided. Americans should remember the example of Spanish legislation. First comes the *ley* (law) and then the *reglamento* (regulation), which sets out all the details. The two are not forthcoming simultaneously. Similarly, the out-

come of negotiation with Spaniards may be general principles
rather than details. Americans who wish to save future head-
aches and/or indulge their passion for detallismo may find
several follow-up meetings to be necessary.

[1] Eduardo Punset, "Porqué no innovan los españoles," *El País*, 8
November 1986.
[2] James A. McCaffrey and Craig R. Haffner, "When Two Cultures
Collide: Doing Business Overseas," *Training and Development
Journal* (October 1985): 26–31.

Encounter Five: **Ir al Grano**

Peter works for the Acme Company at its Minneapolis office. Acme manufactures some of its products in Spain for the European market. Peter is on a trip to Spain, visiting the Spanish operation and looking into the possibility of expanding the manufacturing and distribution activities. The Spanish manager has made contact with several top executives in industry and banking and has arranged meetings with them. How much preliminary general conversation should Peter expect at each meeting?

A. Ten minutes.

B. Twenty minutes.

C. Thirty minutes.

> A. *This would be considered an unreasonably short time unless the Spaniard knows that Americans like to get to the point.*
> B. *This is the average time spent.*
> C. *This is also reasonable.*

Peter's counterpart in his first meeting turns out to have spent his high school junior year in the Twin Cities, so preliminary chat lasts over half an hour. When the topic of the meeting is finally broached, Peter, with an inward sigh of relief, produces the relevant documents. Though a great deal more discussion ensues, Peter is dismayed that many specifics are not addressed. Finally realizing that only twenty minutes of the appointed time remain, Peter starts pressing for firm answers to some of his specific questions. His counterpart answers vaguely and glances at Peter's Spanish manager, who hastily brings the meeting to a close. Can this meeting be considered a success?

> *Yes, for the first meeting. Rapport has been established and the general outlines of the topic have been discussed. There will be time for details later. Nonetheless, if Peter is responsible for those details, in later meetings he will have to insist (politely) on answers, since Spaniards are frequently far more comfortable than Americans with vague generalities.*

6

Play

The Paradox

Both Spaniards and Americans, in Spain and in the United States, comment that while Spaniards work longer days, they seem to have more fun. Spaniards who have moved to the U.S. usually bewail the fact that their lives seem to consist of going from home to work and from work to home. They hark back to the good old days in Spain, while Americans who move back home after living in Spain also complain of the monotony of American life and wax nostalgic for the Spanish lifestyle.

The American passion for detail tends to carry over into social life, so that they plan their play as thoroughly as they plan their work. After work, Americans rush to their next appointments (meetings, sports practice, exercise, etc.) or they rush home to dinner. Spaniards are much less likely to fill their free time with prescheduled events. Spaniards in the United States often comment that in order to get together socially with Americans you have to organize it weeks ahead "and write everything down in a little appointment book."

Many American families try to have dinner at 6:00 even if

they work until 5:00. Since lunch breaks are short and many Americans do not even eat lunch, they are typically very hungry by early evening. In contrast, Spaniards eat a big lunch, so people are not starving in the evening, and in any case *tapas* (snacks) are always available. Even though Spaniards work until 7:00, they meet friends or go shopping after work because dinner can be at any time, and certainly not before 9:00.

Time spent on the typical suburban commute also contributes to the rushed American day. In Spain, even city dwellers do not usually have long commutes because cities are densely populated and well served by public transportation; a Spanish commuter leaving work may face a fifteen-minute subway ride instead of an American's forty-five-minute freeway drive.

Americans living in Spain learn to make less use of their appointment books. New arrivals take a vague "Let's do something on Tuesday night" for a firm commitment and may be annoyed or hurt if nothing materializes when Tuesday night arrives. However, Americans are charmed by the Spanish talent for arranging an outing on the spur of the moment or creating a fiesta out of nothing. This is reflected in the words of Margaret Fountaine, a Victorian traveler and butterfly collector, who visited Spain in the early years of this century.

> The train was more than an hour late, and while we were waiting one man played a guitar, while I, at the urgent request of the assembled company, danced with the *jefe de estación* [stationmaster] in spite of limited space and mountain shoes.[1]

Today's Spanish stations boast high-speed trains, electronic reader boards, and trains that are punctual to the minute; nevertheless, something about Margaret Fountaine's experience still rings true.

It is also easier to be spontaneous with Spaniards because they are not hung up about going to bed early because they have to work the next day. All foreigners (not just Americans) are bemused by the small amount of sleep Spaniards find sufficient. An article once appeared in a Spanish women's magazine discussing stress and simple remedies for dealing with it. On the subject of sleep the advice was *Trata de dormir seis horas* (Make a point of getting six hours' sleep). This implied that even in modern, siesta-less times, six hours' sleep per night, which most Americans would consider to be one or two hours short of the minimum, was regarded by Spaniards as being more than normal and something to strive for. Certainly a Spaniard would never cut short an enjoyable evening in order to go to bed. *Un día es un día* (Live for today), Spaniards say, and it is this attitude that makes Spain fun.

Holidays and Vacations

Spaniards, like many other foreigners, think of the United States as the land of plenty and of opportunity. However, when Spaniards find out about American vacations, they are stunned. The American two-week annual vacation contrasts poorly indeed with the month (not four weeks) that Spaniards, along with other Europeans, expect as their normal due. "Two weeks!" say Spaniards in horror. "How can anyone manage on only two weeks' vacation a year?"

In addition to the annual paid vacation (and to the reduced summer work schedule), Spaniards also enjoy a good number of holidays throughout the year. Religious dates such as Christmas, Good Friday, and Assumption of the Virgin are celebrated throughout Spain. The Easter holiday, famous for the processions in Seville and elsewhere, stretches from Thursday to Sunday or Monday. Cities and regions have their patron saints with corresponding holidays, which vary from one place to another. There are also secular holidays such as Columbus Day and Constitution Day, and all holidays are observed. Americans, accustomed to the flexible observance of holidays in the United States, are disconcerted to find that on Spanish holidays all stores are closed and normal life is completely suspended. Furthermore, in Spain holidays are observed on the actual day they occur. If this falls between Tuesday and Thursday, workers have an opportunity to *hacer puente* (literally, make a bridge). People save up vacation days so that if, for example, a holiday falls on Tuesday, they can make the bridge on Monday, ending up with a four-day break. While the same may be true in the U.S., there are fewer opportunities because Presidents' Day, Memorial Day, and Labor Day are always observed on a Monday.

What is interesting, and for Americans very different, is the way in which Spaniards use their time off. One American man married to a Spanish woman described Spanish leisure in a moment of frustration as "the concept of life as ritual." In the United States, the most ritualized holiday is probably Thanksgiving. Football, turkey, pumpkin pie, and family reunions are the norms of Thanksgiving. No other nonreligious holiday is quite so clearly defined, since at other times one may celebrate or not, get together with the family or not, and eat whatever seems tasty or appropriate. To Americans, it often seems that Spaniards have a Thanksgiving-type ritual for all their holidays. On holidays, as on Sundays, Spaniards get up late, put on their best clothes in late morning, and go out for a walk with the family, which ends with prelunch drinks and snacks at a café. Then comes a big lunch at a restaurant or at the home of a family member, and then everyone watches the movie special on TV or goes out to see a movie or attend some event. Naturally, not every Spaniard spends holidays in this way, but it is overwhelmingly the norm. Many Americans live so far from their families that they cannot possibly spend every Sunday or holiday together. Nor is distance the only factor. Many Americans would regard such close family contact, and particularly spending so much precious free time with family, as an intrusion on their own individuality and their right to spend their holiday as they please. Perhaps it is because Americans have less free time that they often take the attitude that it must be used productively. For Spaniards, free time is not regarded as such a precious commodity, and, in particular, time spent with family is not time to be accounted for.

Social Life

What Spaniards actually do for entertainment in their free time and in socializing with friends is similar to what Americans do: going out for tapas, shopping, sports events, drinks, theater and movies, dinner and dancing. Americans usually have no problem in relating to this, and many an American love affair with Spain (or with a Spaniard) has begun with a social evening.

One feature of Spanish social life which impresses and sometimes embarrasses Americans is the openhanded generosity of Spaniards. Fernando Diaz-Plaja in *The Spaniard and the Seven Deadly Sins* dedicates one short chapter to the sin of avarice, just long enough to say that Spaniards do not suffer from it.[2] This is absolutely true, and nothing shocks a Spaniard more than to see Americans nickeling and diming about who owes what when they are out together. Spaniards are likely to argue about who gets to pick up the whole tab. *"Te invito"* ("You're my guest"), says the Spaniard, snatching up the bill and refusing to allow others to contribute unless it is a very large party. Only Catalans, who have a reputation in Spain for closefistedness, are likely to agree to dividing the bill. Americans sometimes think that Spaniards are trying to show off by making a display of big spending. This is not the case; hospitality in this sense is both generous and reciprocal. I pay for you this time and you pay for me next time.

Generosity extends not only to formal dinners but to something as minor as a cup of coffee or a soft drink. In one of the most common traveler's tales about Spain, the travelers start talking to Spaniards in a bar or restaurant and find when they come to pay that the bill has already been taken care of. This is a basic courtesy in Spain and must be accepted graciously, like invitations to have something to drink. "*¿Quiere tomar algo?*" ("Would you like to have something?") is an automatic question when the conversation is taking place in a café or bar. Business offices have a place to make coffee or will send out for it so that they can offer something to clients when the occasion seems to demand it. For a Spaniard it is next to impossible to say no when someone says "*¿Quiere tomar algo?*" and Americans should also graciously accept when something is offered.

One striking difference between American and Spanish custom is that much if not most of Spanish social life takes place outside the home. Groups of friends who have made arrangements to spend some time together usually meet at a public place such as a café (and every city has cafés that are the favorite meeting places). Then the group goes on to a restaurant, a show, a nightclub, or wherever they have decided. Once again, when a group of Spaniards arranges to meet at a fixed place and time, anything up to an hour may elapse between the arrival of the first person and the arrival of the last. If Americans are involved in one of these groups, they are typically the first to arrive, so they end up waiting the longest until everyone has arrived. Then comes the final straw: one of the Spaniards says "*¿Qué hacemos?*" ("What shall we do?") Much discussion ensues, probably with the Americans glancing at their watches and thinking crossly about the amount of time being wasted. Americans who have adapted to Spain learn to arrive sometime after the fixed hour and to realize that the question "*¿Qué hacemos?*" is largely rhetorical and is asked, even though plans for the evening are already fairly firm, in order to make it clear that any member of the group can still make changes or suggestions.

While Americans might meet at someone's home and go on from there, or maybe go home for coffee or drinks after a social event, Spaniards normally do not expect to go to someone's home for a social gathering. Usually only family members and close friends come to one's home; and parties such as Americans often give are practically unknown. There are several explanations for this: one is the clear division (often attributed to the Moorish influence) in Spain between the privacy of home and the outside world.*

Another reason, which is probably more practical, is that since many Spanish households consist of an extended family, there is not much extra room for inviting people in, and other members of the family may be disturbed by the presence of guests. Finally, Spaniards are house-proud. Only family and intimate friends are allowed to see the debris of normal living. Naturally, this is also true of Americans, who prefer that outsiders not see the house looking like a disaster area, but Spaniards feel more strongly the need to keep up appearances. Americans should respect this and realize that, at least initially, they are unlikely to see the inside of many Spanish homes.

Peace and Quiet versus Ambiente

The bustle of European cities is one of the things that impresses visiting Americans. Spanish cities and towns are no exception. One of the reasons for the activity is the much greater amount of foot traffic in a Spanish city than in an American one. As noted before, Spanish cities are densely built up; almost everyone lives in apartment buildings that have stores and offices on the ground floor. Even small towns and villages are constructed this way, with facades against the sidewalk and any yard space concealed behind the build-

---

* Spaniards change their clothes completely when they get home (instead of just kicking off their shoes, like many Americans). One reason for this is that there is a greater preoccupation with being well turned out when one leaves the house. Clothes worn outside are too good for around the house.

ing. To the visiting Spaniard, an American suburb or small town seems deserted—*No hay nadie en la calle* (There's nobody about), they say. They often feel lonely and are bored at first in American communities, because there is not enough *ambiente*. The literal meaning of this is "atmosphere," but it usually means people and activity.

When Spaniards have nothing to do, they generally go out to do it; when Americans have nothing to do, it seems that they stay home and turn on the TV. The couch potato is an American vegetable; Spaniards with time on their hands change their clothes and go out. Staying home to watch TV is generally a family activity, for example, after the big Sunday lunch.

Other people are an important source of entertainment for Spaniards, who engage in people watching to an extent that Americans find embarrassing. In Spain, watching is not rude at all. Every Spanish apartment, even the poorest, has a balcony from which one can look out. People who sit at sidewalk cafés watch the people walking by, who in turn watch them. When the city is quiet on a Sunday, one has only to go to the nearest seaside or country resort to find all the missing activity, transferred along with the people.

Sports and Hobbies

American sports lovers will find kindred spirits in Spain. On Monday mornings most men on the subway or bus are reading one of the specialized sporting newspapers or the sports section of the daily paper. Weekend afternoons and some weeknights are punctuated by the roars of armchair spectators as their teams score. When there is a really big game, goals are heralded by rockets that are kept in readiness and set off from rooftops or balconies.

Similar also to the United States is the level of sports activity among teenagers. It is only recently that sports have been readily available to all schoolchildren, and particularly to girls. A generation ago sports for girls were virtually unknown. Times have changed and so have attitudes, but Spaniards are still less fitness oriented than Americans, though aerobics and fitness centers have all hit Spain with the same impact as in the U.S.

Hobbies are an area of difference between Spaniards and Americans. For one thing, "hobby" cannot be translated into Castilian except by the word *pasatiempo*, which, like its English counterpart, "pastime," implies not so much a creative and ongoing activity as a pleasant way of spending some odd moments. Spanish people with hobbies usually use the English word to refer to them. There are, as in the United States, collectors of stamps, coins, antiques, and butterflies; nature lovers who pick mushrooms or wild asparagus; hikers and mountain climbers; people who keep pigeons and those who fly gliders. But there are probably fewer craft-type hobbies. A gap has developed between the older generation of women who knitted, crocheted, and sewed (often from necessity) and the younger generation who rarely engage in these pursuits. In the United States, this gap is often filled by crafts such as stenciling, quilt making, weaving, spinning, and so on, but in Spain this is not so. The same applies to home activities such as food preserving or carpentry. In Spain, people feel that it is a waste of time to make something that can easily be bought. Many writers attribute Spanish disrespect for manual skills to the Moorish past. Whether this is a true assessment or not, the fact is that an American who weaves or stencils or does home improvements will be regarded by Spaniards as rather eccentric, perhaps to be admired but not to be emulated.

Clubs and Associations

Local papers in the United States are full of announcements of meetings of clubs and associations, ranging in focus from historical societies to support groups. Furthermore, these clubs are often highly organized, with minutes of each meeting, officers and committees for each activity, and sometimes even an in-house parliamentarian to keep track of the motions, debates, and votes. All this seems to tie in with the American notion of leisure time as something that must be productive.

Spaniards are much less likely to get involved in clubs and associations. There are sporting, social, and professional associations, but not nearly so many as in the United States. Americans sometimes see this as another sign of a lack of community spirit among Spaniards.

It must be remembered that the right to associate was one of the rights that was curtailed, or at least supervised, during the strictest era of the Franco dictatorship. Even with the *apertura* (liberalization) of the early seventies, associations continued to be suspect as possible breeding grounds for dissent; many associations were in fact connected with some kind of ideology. Youth clubs might be closely allied with the church, or hiking clubs with some political movement. The Barcelona Soccer Association (*Club de Futbol Barcelona,* or *Barça*) is famous for having been *més que un club* (more than a club)—a vehicle for Catalan nationalism. At a time when people still were not allowed to speak Catalan and regional autonomy was still a dream, Catalan songs were sung at Barça games, and Barça victories were a source of pride to more than soccer fans. Because of the experience of the last two generations, most Spaniards are not in the habit of belonging to clubs or associations, and, if they thought about it, would probably reject the idea because of not wanting to get involved in something bigger or more complicated than the name and professed aims of the group might suggest.

---

[1] Margaret Fountaine, *Love among the Butterflies* (Harmondsworth, Middlesex: Penguin Books, 1982), 169.

[2] Diaz-Plaja, *Seven Deadly Sins*, 91.

Encounter Six: ¿Qué Hacemos?

David plays volleyball every Saturday with a group of young men (coworkers and their friends). After a few weeks of this, someone proposes that the group get together on Sunday for lunch and a movie afterward. Where will they meet?
  A. At a conveniently located café.
  B. At the restaurant where they will have lunch.
  C. At the home of one of the group members.
  D. At David's home.

   A. *A café is the most likely option.*
   B. *Meeting at the restaurant is possible, but people usually like to get together before lunch for drinks somewhere else.*
   C. *Going to a group member's home is very unlikely. Most young men live at home with their families and would not be comfortable introducing a group of strangers into the privacy of the family home.*
   D. *Although this is a reasonable option, most Spaniards will not expect it.*

COMMENT: The proposal that the group meet for a purpose other than their volleyball game is a sign that the relationship is progressing. If David does propose that the group meet at his home, most Spaniards will be flattered at this sign of confianza.

Epilogue

On the famous Ramblas Avenue in Barcelona stands a fountain, one of many in the old town. Legend has it that a visitor who drinks the water will return to Barcelona.

Spain has captivated generations of Americans for reasons they themselves find hard to enumerate. Spain's society can seem less diverse, work opportunities more limited, politics more tortuous, and cultural life not as exciting as in the United States. Yet Americans find it difficult to leave Spain. And if they do leave, they never forget it.

Américo Castro, one of the great intellectual figures of twentieth-century Spain, begins his *España en su historia* with a chapter on Spaniards' descriptions of themselves. Castro quotes a fifteenth-century writer and diplomat, Fernando de la Torre, who wrote to King Henry IV of Castile in 1455.

Fernando de la Torre (the Spanish ambassador to the French court) attempts to describe...what Spain is like and how it appears in comparison with other nations.... "Spain's worth resides in what it *is*, much less than in what it produces by the labor of its people."

Resources

The following is a brief listing of material available in the United States that offers an introduction to Spain or to cross-cultural communication and adaptation.

Books

A wealth of material is published in English, the greater part of it consisting of scholarly works or tourist guides. Some books of general interest are listed below; for an excellent, comprehensive catalogue, the reader is referred to Amazon.com, the on-line bookseller (www.amazon.com).

Brenan, Gerald. *The Spanish Labyrinth: An Account of the Social and Political Background of the Spanish Civil War.* New York: Cambridge University Press, 1990.

First published in 1943, this remains one of the classic studies of the Spanish Civil War.

Carr, Raymond. *Modern Spain, 1875–1980.* London: Oxford University Press, 1980.

A compact and readable overview of modern Spanish political history. Carr, a well-known scholar, traces successive periods of Spanish history as the country searches for legitimate and stable government.

Cohen, David, and Rick Smolan. *A Day in the Life of Spain.* San Francisco: Collins, 1988.

Beautiful photographs capture moments in the daily lives of a wide variety of Spaniards in every possible setting. These photographs are especially useful because they record the contemporary scene.

Gilmour, David. *Cities of Spain.* Chicago: Ivan R. Dee, 1992.

Vivid portraits of the history, architecture, festivals, and particular character of nine major Spanish cities. We suggest that Gilmour be read in conjuntion with Robert Kern's book, *The Regions of Spain,* listed below.

Hooper, John. *The New Spaniards.* New York: Penguin USA, 1995.

John Hooper is an English journalist who spent a number of years as the correspondent in Spain and Portugal for the British daily, *The Guardian.* He has produced a comprehensive and readable study of the transition to democracy after 1975.

Kern, Robert W. *The Regions of Spain.* Westport, CT: Greenwood, 1995.

A complete and richly illustrated reference book on Spain, organized by region and province and covering history, economy, literature, art, music, social customs, historic sites, and cuisine.

Kohls, L. Robert. *Survival Kit for Overseas Living.* 3d ed. Yarmouth, ME: Intercultural Press, 1996.

This deceptively slim book explains the basic concepts of culture and cross-cultural adaptation in layman's language, enhanced by guidelines, checklists, and exercises.

Michener, James A. *Iberia: Spanish Travels and Reflections*. New York: Fawcett Crest, 1968.

This is one of James Michener's best-known and best-loved books. Three decades have rendered much of the social and political commentary obsolete. However, the book is valuable for its combination of history and personal observation, covering twelve distinct cities and regions. Michener's prose is as readable as ever, and his love of Spain is evident on every page.

Storti, Craig. *The Art of Crossing Cultures*. Yarmouth, ME: Intercultural Press, 1990.

Craig Storti presents a model for the process of adapting to another culture. He explains the kinds of adjustments to be made, problems that can arise, and a technique for adapting successfully. This gracefully written book is enhanced with quotations from an array of literary sources.

Films

NOTE: The films in this section are sometimes shown in the United States at specialty theaters; they are also available on video, subtitled in English.

Almodóvar, Pedro.

Many Americans are familiar with *Woman on the Verge of a Nervous Breakdown*, which enjoyed great popularity in the United States. Almodóvar is the most prolific of the current directors, producing a film a year in his characteristic style—zany, sometimes weird, and frequently outrageous. Among his titles are *Dark Habits, The Law of Desire, Matador, What Have I Done to Deserve This?, Tie Me Up! Tie Me Down!, Labyrinth of Passion, High Heels, Kika,* and *The Flower of My Secret.*

Aragón, Manuel Gutiérrez.

Demons in the Garden (1982) and Half of Heaven (1988) are social narratives like Carlos Saura's films of the 1970s, but with fewer sinister undercurrents. Things I Left in Havana (1997) continues the tradition, looking at Cuban immigrants.

Betancor, Antonio.

Valentina (1984) and Crónica del Alba (1990) are coming-of-age stories based on the novels of Ramón Sender.

Buñuel, Luis.

The father of modern Spanish cinema first made his name with the surreal Un chien andalou. He worked from exile in France, and many of his films were banned in Spain. His only film currently available in the United States is Viridiana (1961).

Erice, Victor.

Erice directed The Spirit of the Beehive (1973), a lyrical portrait of childhood and traditional village life.

Saura, Carlos.

Saura was one of the most prolific and influential directors of the 1970s. Films such as The Garden of Delights (1970), Cría (1977), and Mama Turns 100 (1979) chronicle family and social relationships. In the 1980s Saura made his "Dance Trilogy" in collaboration with the Antonio Gades flamenco dance troupe: Carmen, based on the Bizet opera; Blood Wedding, based on the play by Federico García Lorca; and El Amor Brujo, based on music by Manuel de Falla. In the 1990s Saura has made Ay, Carmela!, set in the Civil War, and Sevillanas, another dance movie.

Trueba, Fernando.

Belle Epoque, set in the Civil War, was released in the United States in 1993 and won the Academy Award for Best Foreign Film.

The success of *Belle Epoque* combined with the popularity of Almodóvar to whet the appetite of international filmgoers for Spanish films. A new generation of Spanish filmmakers is taking advantage of improved funding and distribution with a new crop of films each year. Some are available on video, while others can be seen at film festivals.

Docudramas based on real-life deadly love triangles.
Aranda, Vicente   *Lovers: A True Story* (1991)
                         Intruso (1993)
Franco, Ricardo   *Lucky Star* (1997)

The story of women fighting in the Civil War.
Aranda, Vicente   *Libertarias* (1995)

Satire on the workings of the family.
León de Aranoa, Fernando *Familia* (1997)

Contemporary dramas of greed and success, crime and punishment.
Barroso, Mariano   *Ecstasy* (1996)
Carparsoro, Daniel   *Blinded* (1997)

Growing up in the late Franco era.
Armendáriz, Montxo   *Secrets of the Heart* (1997)
Garcia, José Luis   *Tramway to Malvarossa* (1996)
Martínez-Lázaro, Emilio *Backroads* (1997)

Glossary

Words

abrazo: hug (*Un abrazo*: informal ending for letters)

acoso sexual: sexual harassment

adiós: good-bye/go with God

ahora: now

allioli: garlic mayonnaise

ambiente: atmosphere

apertura: liberalization; literally "opening"

beso: kiss (*Besos*: informal ending for letters—women only)

blanco: white

buenos días: good morning

buenas tardes: good afternoon

castellano: Castilian; also Latin American variety of Spanish language

catedrático: tenured professor

cava: Catalan champagne

civismo: good citizenship

Comité de empresa: employees' council
confianza: trust
convenio: job agreement
copiar: copying
cortes: parliament
desconocido: stranger
detallismo: detail consciousness
discusión: argument
doble jornada: double shift
egoismo: egotism
el gordo: the big one
enchufe: contacts
envidia: jealousy, envy
escándalo público: public scandal
Estatuto del trabajador: workers' code
familia: family
familia política: in-laws
franquismo: the Franco era
ganster: gangster
gansterismo: lawlessness
hablando fuerte: talking loudly
hacer el ridículo: to look foolish
hacer puente: to make a bridge
Hacienda: the Spanish Treasury
hidalgo: literally, the son of somebody; a gentleman
hola: hello
horario de verano: summer schedule
insolidarios: lacking in solidarity
jefe de estación: stationmaster

la madre patria: the mother country

Levante: Mediterranean coast

ley: law

machismo: male sexist behavior

machista: male chauvinist

maleducado: rude, boorish, bad mannered

mañana: tomorrow

menú del día: daily special

meseta: high plateau

mili: military service

natural de…: native of…

pasatiempo: pastime

paseo: stroll

pícaro: rascal

pijo: spoiled rich kid

piropo: compliment or comment about appearance

portero: doorman

reglamento: regulation; the section of Spanish legislation
specifying details accompanying certain laws

Reyes Católicos: Catholic Monarchs

señora: title for a married or older woman

señorita: title for an unmarried or younger woman

suecas: Swedish women

suerte: luck

tapas: varied snacks to accompany drinks

tertulia: circle of friends, typically men, who meet regularly in
the same bar or restaurant/also radio and TV talk shows

tú: informal form of "you"

urbanización: modern housing development

usted: polite form of "you"

132

Expressions

Aqui hay blancos, negritos, y negritos con cualificaciones: In this
company there are white folks, darkies, and darkies with
qualifications

Club de Futbol Barcelona: the Barcelona Soccer Association

¿Con quién tengo que hablar?: Who do I need to talk to?

el prolijo detallismo de los americanos: the Americans' unlimited passion for details

Es igual: It's all the same

faltar al respeto: to be lacking in respect

¡Haberlo dicho?: Why didn't you say something before?

Hablando, la gente se entiende: Discussion is the way to understanding

Hecha la ley, hecha la trampa: Every law has its loophole

ir al grano: to get to the point

leyenda negra: evil legend

més que un club: more than a club

No hay nadie en la calle: There's nobody about

Obedezco, pero no cumplo: I obey but do not comply

por regla general: as a general rule

Prohibido cantar: No singing

¿Qué hacemos?: What shall we do?

¿Quiere tomar algo?: Would you like to have something (to
drink)?

Respeten el descanso de los vecinos: Respect the sleep of our
neighbors

Somos comodones: We like things easy

Somos el vagón de la cola: We always bring up the rear

Te invito: You're my guest

Trata de dormir seis horas: Make a point of getting six hours' sleep

Un día es un día: Live for today

una persona de confianza: one who can be trusted

Vive de tus padres hasta que puedas vivir de tus hijos: Live off your parents until you can live off your children

Ya me lo pagará mañana: You can pay me tomorrow

Ya nos conocemos: We know each other